REVELATION 1:18

THE ALPHA AND OMEGA

"Outline Studies of the Book of Revelation"

By

Dr. Paul W. Noe

DEDICATION

I affectionately dedicate this book to Rev. Ray Talley and Dr. Tom Patterson. These two men of God are my spiritual fathers in the ministry. They have loved me, prayed for me, supported me, encouraged me, given me opportunities to preach, and helped me all my ministry. Their influence has made a tremendous impact upon my life. Their investment in my ministry is invaluable.

Rev. Ray Talley and Paul Noe in Hendersonville, North Carolina
(Rev. Ray Talley was my pastor as a teenager.
He also officiated my ordination service on June 16, 1985.)

Dr. Tom Patterson and Paul Noe in Rock Hill, South Carolina
(I served under Dr. Patterson from 1984-1987 as Associate Pastor and Minister of Youth at Woodhaven Baptist Church. He also married my wife, Bobbi, and me on August 10, 1985.)

THE ALPHA AND OMEGA

A WORD FROM THE AUTHOR

Dear Friends,

Eschatology (the study of end time events) is a very interesting and important subject. We are certainly living in the last days. As Christians we are anticipating the return of our Lord and Savior Jesus Christ. We are commanded to *"watch"* for His arrival. Jesus said in **Matthew 25:13**, "Watch therefore, for ye know neither the day nor the hour wherein the Son of man cometh." KJV **Titus 2:13** also declares, "Looking for that blessed hope, and the glorious appearing of the great God and our Savior Jesus Christ." KJV

The book of Revelation is both fascinating and complicated. By taking the word, *"WATCH,"* we will investigate five major themes of Revelation. They are as followings:

W – ORSHIP – Revelation 1, 5
A – SSEMBLIES (Churches) – Revelation 2, 3
T – RIBULATION – Revelation 4 - 18
C – ONQUEST – Revelation 19
H – EAVEN – Revelation 21, 22

I have entitled this book, *THE ALPHA AND OMEGA.* Jesus states that He is *"The Alpha and Omega"* three times in the book of Revelation (Revelation 1:8, 21:6, and 22:13). *Alpha* is the first letter of the Greek alphabet and *Omega* is the last letter of the Greek alphabet. Jesus is the commencement and consummation of eternity.

This book is not intended to be an exhausted commentary on the book of Revelation. It is only an overview. It is meant to be utilized with your open Bible as you follow the outlines for each chapter. I hope this study of Revelation will be informative, edifying, and beneficial. May you be blessed as you investigate the pages of Revelation for yourself. Keep worshiping, working, witnessing, and waiting until He comes.

Dr. Paul W. Noe
Sweetwater Baptist Church
198 Sweetwater Road
North Augusta, South Carolina 29860
(803) 279-2821

SPECIAL ACKNOWLEDGEMENT

The picture of the *"Alpha and Omega"* stained-glass window on the cover of this book is located at the First Christian Church in Belvedere, South Carolina. It is in honor and memory of "Hazel S. Johnson." A special "thanks" goes out to Ray and Judy Johnson and Junior Johnson for allowing me to photograph this beautiful window. Hazel S. Johnson is the mother of Ray Johnson and grandmother of Junior Johnson.

"Major Events of the End Times"

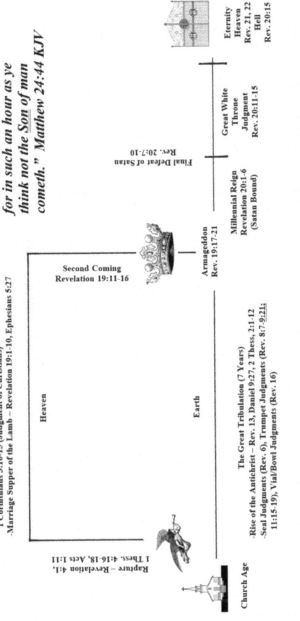

"Therefore be ye also ready: for in such an hour as ye think not the <u>Son</u> of man cometh." Matthew 24:44 KJV

-Judgment Seat of Christ – Romans 14:10, 2 Corinthians 5:10, 1 Corinthians 3:10-15 (Judgment of Christians)
-Marriage Supper of the Lamb – Revelation 19:1-10, Ephesians 5:27

Heaven

Second Coming
Revelation 19:11-16

Armageddon
Rev. 19:17-21

Final Defeat of Satan
Rev. 20:7-10

Great White Throne Judgment
Rev. 20:11-15

Eternity
Heaven
Rev. 21, 22
Hell
Rev. 20:15

Millennial Reign
Revelation 20:1-6
(Satan Bound)

Earth

The Great Tribulation (7 Years)
-Rise of the Antichrist – Rev. 13, Daniel 9:27, 2 Thess, 2:1-12
-Seal Judgments (Rev. 6), Trumpet Judgments (Rev. 8:7-9:21; 11:15-19), Vial/Bowl Judgments (Rev. 16)

Rapture – Revelation 4:1, 1 Thess, 4:16-18, Acts 1:11

Church Age

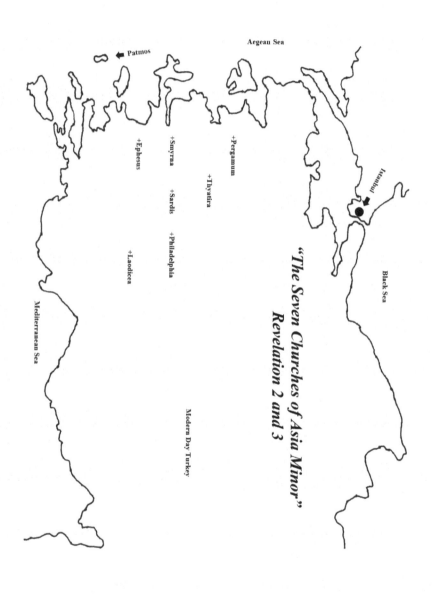

Aegean Sea

Patmos

+Pergamum

+Thyatira

+Ephesus

+Smyrna

+Sardis

+Philadelphia

+Laodicea

Istanbul

Black Sea

"The Seven Churches of Asia Minor"
Revelation 2 and 3

Modern Day Turkey

Mediterranean Sea

"THE BOOK OF REVELATION"
INTRODUCTION

*The word, *"Revelation,"* means "an uncovering," "an unveiling," or "a disclosure."[1]

*The Apostle John received this Revelation while banished on the Isle of Patmos for his faith in the Lord Jesus Christ (Revelation 1:9). The island is approximately twenty-five miles in circumference and is off the coast of Asia Minor. It has a barren and mountainous terrain formed by volcanoes. Ecclesiastical tradition says that John was forced to work in the mines of Patmos.[2]

*The Book of Revelation is an unveiling of the person of the Lord Jesus Christ and His plans for the future (Revelation 1:7).

"Revelation is the climax of the Bible, the fulfillment of what God started in Genesis." **Warren W. Wiersbe[3]**

*It was written approximately 95 or 96 A. D. during the reign of the Roman ruler Domitian.[4]

*John wrote this book to encourage persecuted Christians that Christ would ultimately defeat Satan and reign for eternity as *"King of kings and Lord of lords."*

*Revelation contains a promise to those who read it and obey it (Revelation 1:3).

***Numbers** are very significant in Revelation. For example, the number 7 is used throughout the book. It is symbolic of perfection and completion (Seven churches – Revelation 1:20, Seven Seals – Revelation 5:1, Seven Trumpets – Revelation 8:2, Seven Vials/Bowls – Revelation 15:7, etc.)

***Two openings in Heaven:**
1. **Rapture – Revelation 4:1**
2. **Glorious Return – Revelation 19:11**

GENESIS AND REVELATION

Genesis – The Commencement of Heaven and Earth (1:1);
Revelation – The Consummation of Heaven and Earth (21:1).

Genesis – The Entrance of Sin and the Curse (3:1-19);
Revelation – The End of Sin and the Curse (21:27; 22:3).

1

Genesis – The Dawn of Satan and His Activities (3:1-7);
Revelation – The Doom of Satan and His Activities (20:10).

Genesis – The Tree of Life Relinquished (2:9; 3:24);
Revelation – The Tree of Life Regained (22:2).

Genesis – Death Makes its Entrance (2:17; 5:5);
Revelation – Death Makes Its Exit (21:4).

Genesis – Sorrow Begins (3:16);
Revelation – Sorrow is Banished (21:4).[5]

OUTLINE OF THE BOOK OF REVELATION
The Outline is Found in Revelation 1:19

I. PAST THINGS – Chapter 1
"Things which thou hast seen"
*John had a vision of the glorified Christ.
  A. **His Deity** – Revelation 1:8 – *"Almighty"*
  B. **His Sovereignty** – Revelation 1:8
     "Alpha and Omega, the beginning and the ending"
  C. **His Ministry** – Revelation 1:13
     *Reference to the Old Testament Priest
     "Clothed with a garment down to the foot"
     "Golden girdle"
  D. **His Purity** – Revelation 1:14
     *"His head and his hairs were white like wool, as white as
     snow"* – Revelation 1:14
     "His countenance was as the sun" – Revelation 1:16
  E. **His Authority** – Revelation 1:12-17
     "Eyes were as a flame of fire" – verse 14
     "Feet like fine brass" – verse 15
     "Voice as the sound of many waters" – verse 15
     "He had in his right hand seven stars" – verse 16
     "Out of his mouth went a sharp two-edged sword" –
     verse 16

F. His Victory – Revelation 1:5, 18
   "Keys of hell and death"

II. PRESENT THINGS – Chapters 2 and 3
   "Things which are"
   *The **"Seven"** churches are representative of the church throughout church history. The messages to these specific churches are applicable to any church experiencing similar circumstances.
   *Warren W. Wiersbe describes these churches as follows:
   A. Ephesus – Revelation 2:1-7
      "The Backslidden Church"
   B. Smyrna – Revelation 2:8-11
      "The Suffering Church"
   C. Pergamos – Revelation 2:12-17
      "The Worldly Church"
   D. Thyatira – Revelation 2:18-29
      "The Unrepentant Church"
   E. Sardis – Revelation 3:1-6
      "The Dying Church"
   F. Philadelphia – Revelation 3:7-13
      "The Serving Church"
   G. Laodicea – Revelation 3:14-22
      "The Apostate Church"[6]

III. PROPHECTICAL THINGS – Chapters 4-22
   "Things which shall be hereafter"
   A. Exaltation (Worship of the Lamb) - Revelation 4:1-5:14
   B. Tribulation – Revelation 6:1-18:24
      *John MacArthur describes the Tribulation Period as follows:
      "The Tribulation refers to that seven-year time period immediately following the Rapture - removal of the church from the earth (John 14:1-3; 1 Thess. 4:13-18), when the righteous judgments of God will be poured out upon an unbelieving world (Jer. 30:7; Dan. 9:27; 12:1; 2 Thess. 2:7-12; Rev. 16). These judgments will be climaxed by the return of Christ in glory to the earth (Matt. 24:27-31; 25:31-46; 2 Thess. 2:7-12)."[7]

3

*The Tribulation Period will be a time of . . .
1. Calamity (Disaster)
2. Chaos (Disorder)
3. Catastrophe
4. Confusion
5. Crisis
6. Condemnation (Judgment of God)
7. Conflict (War)
8. Carnage (Death)

C. **Consummation**
   *God's plan for the ages is consummated in Revelation.
   1. The Return of the Glorified King – Revelation 19:1-21
   2. The Millennium – Revelation 20:1-10
      "The Latin word means 'thousand years.' It is used for the thousand-year reign of Christ spoken of in Rev. 20:1-6, in which prophecies like Is: 2:2-4; 11:6-9, and Rom. 8:19-23 will be fulfilled."
      The Believer's Study Bible[8]
   3. The Great White Throne Judgment – Revelation 20:11-15
   4. The Eternal State – Revelation 21:1-22:21

"THE REVELATION OF JESUS CHRIST"
Revelation 1:4-18

*John has a revelation and vision of the Lord Jesus Christ.

1. John's Affliction – verse 9 – *"tribulation"*
   *John was banished to the Island of Patmos for his faith in the Lord Jesus Christ.

2. John's Attitude – verse 10
   "I was in the Spirit on the Lord's day"
   *When we worship, we must be in the Spirit.
   "God is a Spirit: and they that worship him must worship him in spirit and in truth." **John 4:24 KJV**

3. John's Assignment – verses 11, 19
   *John was instructed to write the vision down.
   *His manuscript is the *Book of Revelation* in our Bibles.

*This vision helps us to get a glimpse of Jesus.

I. PERSON – verse 8 – He is God

*He is the *"ALMIGHTY"*

"In the beginning was the Word, and the Word was with God, and the Word was God." **John 1:1 KJV**

"I and my Father are one." **John 10:30 KJV**

"He is the sole expression of the glory of God-the Light-being, the out-raying of the divine – and He is the perfect imprint and very image of [God's] nature, upholding and maintaining and guiding and propelling the universe by His mighty word of power. When He had by offering Himself accomplished our cleansing of sins and riddance of guilt, He sat down at the right hand of the divine Majesty on high."
Hebrews 1:3 Amplified

II. POWER – verses 5, 18 – Jesus has conquered death.

*The resurrection is the greatest of all miracles.

"And what is the exceeding greatness of his power to us ward who believe, according to the working of his mighty power, Which he wrought in Christ, when he raised him from the dead, and set him at his own right hand in the heavenly places." **Ephesians 1:19, 20 KJV**

III. POSITION – verse 5 – *"Prince of the kings of the earth"*

*Jesus is ROYALTY.

*He is both a Prince (Isaiah 9:6) and King (Revelation 17:14).

". . . He who is the blessed and only Potentate, the King of kings and Lord of lords." **1 Timothy 6:15 NKJV**

IV. PASSION – verse 5 – *"Loved Us"*

*Jesus loves us.

"Greater love hath no man than this, that a man lay down his life for his friends." **John 15:13 KJV**

*Jesus loves us so much He was willing to die for us.

"But God demonstrates his own love for us in this: While we were still sinners, Christ died for us."
Romans 5:8 NIV

V. PARDON – verse 5 – *"Washed us from our sins in his own blood"*

"In whom we have redemption through his blood, the forgiveness of sins, according to the riches of his grace." **Ephesians 1:7 KJV**

"But if we walk in the light, as he is in the light, we have fellowship one with another, and the blood of Jesus Christ his Son cleanseth us from all sin." **1 John 1:7 KJV**

VI. PROMISE – verse 7 – *"Cometh with clouds"*

*Jesus is coming again.

*The Second Coming of Christ is one of the great doctrines of the Bible.

"Looking for that blessed hope, and the glorious appearing of the great God and our Savior Jesus Christ." **Titus 2:13 KJV**

VII. PROCLAMATION – verse 8, 11

*Jesus refers to Himself as the *"Alpha and Omega."*

*Alpha is the first letter of the Greek Alphabet

*Omega is the last letter of the Greek Alphabet

*This proclamation is a reference to the eternal nature of the Lord Jesus Christ.

"Jesus Christ the same yesterday, and today, and forever." **Hebrews 13:8 KJV**

VIII. PURITY – verse 14

*Christ is holy. Holiness is an essential attribute of the deity of the Lord Jesus.

"For such an high priest became us, who is holy, harmless, undefiled, separate from sinners, made higher than the heavens." **Hebrews 7:26 KJV**

"Who did no sin, neither was guile found in his mouth." **1 Peter 2:22 KJV**

*Jesus Christ is sinless and perfect.

"And ye know that he was manifested to take away our sins; and in him is no sin." **1 John 3:5 KJV**

"Immortal, invisible, God only wise,
In light inaccessible hid from our eyes,

Most blessed, most glorious, the Ancient of Days,
Almighty, victorious, Thy great name we praise. "
Walter Chalmers Smith[9]

"THE SEVEN CHURCHES OF ASIA MINOR"

*God sends the messages to the seven churches on three different levels.

1. Pastor – Revelation 1:20
2. People – Congregation
3. Personally – To Each Person

*Many scholars and Bible teachers believe that the seven churches represent periods in church history.

****William McDonald** in the ***Believer's Bible Commentary*** describes these periods of history as follows:

Ephesus: The church of the first century was Generally praiseworthy but it had already left its first love.

Smyrna: From the first to the fourth century, the church suffered persecution under the Roman emperors.

Pergamos: During the fourth and fifth centuries, Christianity was recognized as an official religion through Constantine's patronage.

Thyatira: From the sixth to the fifteenth century, the Roman Catholic Church largely held sway in Western Christendom until rocked by the Reformation. In the East, the Orthodox Church ruled.

Sardis: The sixteenth and seventeenth centuries were the post-Reformation period. The light of the Reformation soon became dim.

Philadelphia: During the eighteenth and nineteenth centuries, there were mighty revivals and great missionary movements.

Laodicea: The church of the last days is pictured as lukewarm and apostate. It is the church of liberalism and ecumenism.[10]

"THE CHURCH AT EPHESUS"
Revelation 2:1-7

*Ephesus
1. In ancient inscriptions Ephesus was described as the *"First and Greatest Metropolis of Asia."*[11]
2. Ephesus was a commercial center and located on a major trade route.
3. A temple dedicated to Diana (Artemis) was located in Ephesus. This structure was one of the seven wonders of the ancient world (Acts 19:35).[12]
4. The city had an extremely large theater that would accommodate approximately 25,000 persons.[13]
5. Ephesus had a beautiful library known as the Celsus Library.[14]

*We know more about Ephesus than any of the other seven churches mentioned in the Book of Revelation.
1. Aquila and Priscilla helped to instruct Apollos concerning the Word of God in Ephesus – Acts 18:24-28
2. Certain disciples were filled with the Holy Spirit there – Acts 19:1-7
3. The Apostle Paul preached in the synagogue of the Jew in Ephesus for three months – Acts 19:8
4. After opposition from the Jews, Paul moved to the School of Tyrannus. He preached in this location for two years – Acts 19:9-12
5. There was an amazing encounter with the Sons of Sceva and a demon possessed man in Ephesus (Acts 19:13-20). A great revival and book burning took place as a result.
6. Demetrius the silversmith led a great uproar against Paul in Ephesus – Acts 19:21-41

*God used the Apostle Paul in a mighty way in the city of Ephesus.
"And God wrought special miracles by the hands of Paul: so that from his body were brought unto the sick handkerchiefs and aprons, and the diseases went out of them, and the evil spirits went out of them." **Acts 19:11, 12 KJV**
"And this was known to all the Jews and Greeks also dwelling at Ephesus; and fear fell on them all, and the name of the Lord Jesus was magnified." **Acts 19:17 KJV**

"And so mightily grew the Word of God, and prevailed."
Acts 19:20 KJV
*Thirty years later God sends a message to the church at Ephesus
and tells them that they need a revival.
*Note the **Sender of the Letter** – Jesus Christ
1. **The Power of Christ** – verses 1, 1:20 – *"Holdeth"*
   *Picture of Authority
2. **The Presence of Christ** – verse 1 – *"Walketh"*

*Notice four things about the Church at Ephesus in this
passage.

I. THE RECOGNITION – verses 2, 3, 6
*Jesus recognizes several wonderful areas and fruits in this
church.
A. Their Works and Labor – verses 2, 3
   *This was a hard-working congregation.
B. Their Patience – verses 2, 3 – enduring, consistent, and
   determined.
C. Their Purity – verse 2
   "Canst not bear them which are evil"
D. Their Sound Doctrine – verse 2
   *"Thou hast tried them which say they are apostles, and are
   not, and hast found them liars."*
   "Nicolaitanes" – verse 6 – Apparently, a sect which
   advocated license in matters of Christian behavior,
   including free love.[15]

II. THE REBUKE – verse 4
"Thou hast left thy first love"
*They had lost their passion for God. They were going through
the motions.
*God wants us to love him beyond all else.
*Love reveals loyalty – Simon Peter – John 21:15-19
A. We are to Love God Personally
   "If ye love me, keep my commandments."
   John 14:15 KJV
   *Christianity is a personal love relationship with God.
B. We are to Love God Supremely

"And thou shalt love the Lord thy God with all thy heart, and with all thy soul, and with all thy mind, and with all thy strength." **Mark 12:30 KJV**
*The Lord is to be the love of your life.

III. THE REMEDY – verse 5
*The cure is twofold:
A. Remember
*To consider how it used to be.
*Memory is a good thing.
*It is too easy to forget the blessings and goodness of God.
B. Repent
*Turn from your wicked ways.
"Let the wicked forsake his way, and the unrighteous man his thoughts: and let him return unto the Lord, and he will have mercy upon him; and to our God, for he will abundantly pardon." **Isaiah 55:7 KJV**

IV. THE REWARD – verse 7
*God promises a reward to those who overcome.
A. The Prerequisite of the Reward –
"Overcome"
*We can overcome daily and ultimately.
B. The Possession of the Reward – *"Tree of Life"*
*Reference to eternal life – Genesis 2:9, 3:22-24
*In the Garden of Eden the Tree of Life was relinquished, but in Heaven the Tree of Life will be regained (Revelation 22:2).

"My Jesus I love Thee,
I know Thou art mine.
For Thee all the follies
of sin I resign.
My gracious redeemer,
My Saviour art Thou
If ever I loved Thee,
my Jesus 'tis now."
William R. Featherstone[16]

"THE CHURCH AT SMYRNA"
Revelation 2:8-11

*There are only two churches out of seven in the Book of Revelation that are not rebuked – Philadelphia and Smyrna.

*Smyrna
1. Sea Port town located about 35 miles north of Ephesus.
2. It was a major center for the imperial Caesar-cult in the ancient world.[17]
3. It was famous for science, medicine, and the majesty of its buildings.[18]
4. Received its name from one of its principal commercial products – myrrh.

    "Smyrna" – "Bitterness"

    *Myrrh was made from a gum resin/sap taken from a shrubby tree that had a bitter taste.

    *Myrrh was used for the following:
    A. Ingredient in making perfume (Psalm 45:8)
    B. Ingredient in the anointing oil of the priest (Exodus 30:23)
    C. Purification of women (Esther 2:12)
    D. Embalming (John 19:39)[19]
       *One of the Christmas gifts that the wise men gave Jesus was myrrh – Matthew 2:11
5. We do not know the circumstances in which the church at Smyrna was established.
6. We do know that Smyrna was a difficult place in which to maintain a Christian testimony because the church there was under great persecution and affliction.

I. THE AUTHOR – verse 8
*The author is the Lord Jesus Christ.
A. <u>His Character</u> – *"First and the Last"*
*Christ is the one who holds everything together.
"For by him were all things created, that are in heaven, and that are in earth, visible and invisible, whether they be thrones, or dominions, or principalities, or powers: all things were created by him and for him: and he is before all things, and by him all things consist."
Colossians 1:16, 17 KJV

B. <u>His Conquest</u> – *"which was dead, and is alive!"*
  *Christ has conquered death.
  "For to this end Christ both died, and rose, and revived, that
  he might be Lord both of the dead and living."
  Romans 14:9 KJV
  "But is now made manifest by the appearing of our Savior
  Jesus Christ, who hath abolished death, and hath brought
  life and immortality to light through the gospel."
  2 Timothy 1:10 KJV

II. THE AFFLICTION
  *This church was suffering under great affliction.
  A. <u>The Perception</u> – verse 9 – *"I know"*
    *The Lord knows all things.
    "For God is not unrighteous to forget your work and labour
    of love, which ye have ministered to the saints, and do
    minister." **Hebrews 6:10 KJV**
  B. <u>The Performance</u> – verse 9 – *"works"*
    *This was a hard-working church.
    "Let your light so shine before men, that they may see your
    good works, and glorify your Father which is in heaven."
    Matthew 5:17 KJV
  C. <u>The Persecution</u> - verses 9, 10 – *"Tribulation"*
    "Ten Day" – may refer to ten separate attempts to wipe out
    Christianity prompted by the law of ten different Roman
    rulers.[20]
    *Christians are not immune to persecution and tribulation.
    "Blessed are ye, when men shall revile you, and persecute
    you, and shall say all manner of evil against you falsely,
    for my sake. Rejoice, and be exceeding glad: for great is
    your reward in heaven: for so persecuted they the prophets
    which were before you." **Matthew 5:11, 12 KJV**
    "Yea, and all that will live godly in Christ Jesus shall suffer
    persecution." **2 Timothy 3:12 KJV**
  D. <u>The Poverty</u> – verse 9 - *"Poverty, (but thou art rich)"*
    *They were poor physically, but rich spiritually.
    *In Christ you are rich!!
    *Heaven, peace, love, joy, eternal life makes us rich.

"As sorrowful, yet always rejoicing; as poor, yet making many rich; as nothing, and yet possessing all things."
2 Corinthians 6:10 KJV

"For ye know the grace of our Lord Jesus Christ, that, though he was rich, yet for your sakes he became poor, that ye through his poverty might be rich."
2 Corinthians 8:9 KJV

E. <u>The Pretenders</u> – **verse 9**

*Christ knew who the pretenders were.

*He recognizes imposters.

*You cannot pretend to be something that you are not before God.

*He sees the heart and what is on the inside.

"I the Lord search the heart, I try the reins, even to give every man according to his ways, and according to the fruit of his doings." **Jeremiah 17:10 KJV**

III. **THE APPEAL** – verse 10 – *"Be faithful unto death"*

*As Christians we are to be faithful.

"Moreover it is required in stewards, that a man be found faithful." **1 Corinthians 4:2 KJV**

*Are you willing to lay down your life for the sake of the gospel?

*Take a stand for Christ. Do not be ashamed of Jesus.

"Whosoever therefore shall confess me before men, him will I confess also before my Father which is in heaven. But whosoever shall deny me before men, him will I also deny before my Father which is in heaven."
Matthew 10:32, 33 KJV

*The Bible is filled with those who gave their lives for the Lord.

1. John the Baptist – Mark 6:27
2. Stephen – Acts 7:58
3. James – Acts 12:2

IV. **THE AWARD** – verse 10 – *"Crown of Life"*

*A Crown of Life is promised to faithful believers.

*Numerous crowns mentioned in the Bible.

A. <u>**Crown of Righteousness**</u> – 2 Timothy 4:8

B. <u>Crown of Glory</u> – 1 Peter 5:4
C. <u>Crown of Life</u> – James 1:12, Revelation 2:10
D. <u>Incorruptible Crown</u> – 1 Corinthians 9:25
*These crowns will not be worn on our heads in heaven, but to be presented to our blessed Lord – Revelation 4:10, 11

"Crown Him with many crowns
The Lamb upon the throne
Hark How the heav'nly anthems drowns
All music but its own!
Awake, my soul And sing
Of Him Who died for thee
And hail Him as thy matchless King
Thru all eternity."
Matthew Bridges[21]

"THE CHURCH AT PERGAMOS/PERGAMUM"
Revelation 2:12-17

*Pergamos – (Pergamum)
1. Twenty miles from the sea.
2. Capital city of Mysia.
3. It was known for its wealth and fashion.
4. Pergamos was the site of the first temple to the Caesar-cult.[22]
5. Zeus and Athena were also worshipped in Pergamos.[23]
6. Parchment was invented in Pergamos.[24]
7. The city contained a massive library that rival Alexandria.[25]

*This church needed to be reminded of the authority of Christ.

*Verse 12 – *"These things saith he which hath the sharp sword with two edges."*

1. **The Authority of the Savior**
   *Jesus has authority!
   "I am he that liveth, and was dead; and, behold, I am alive for evermore, Amen; and have the keys of hell and death."
   ### Revelation 1:18 KJV
   "Then Jesus came to them and said, All authority in heaven and on earth has been given to me." **Matthew 28:18 NIV**

2. **The Authority of the Scriptures**
   "Sharp sword with two edges"

14

*Reference to the authority of the Word of God!

"For the Word of God is quick, and powerful, and sharper than any twoedged sword, piercing even to the dividing asunder of soul and spirit, and of the thoughts and intents of the heart." **Hebrews 4:12 KJV**

"And take the helmet of salvation, and the sword of the spirit, which is the word of God." **Ephesians 6:17 KJV**

I. THE CHURCH
A. <u>The Place of the Church</u>
*Paul passed through this province, embarking at the port of Troas, on his first voyage to Europe (Acts 16:7, 8).

*Pergamos was a great city, but a difficult one to be a Christian in.

*Pergamos was known chiefly for its many religions.

1. Temple dedicated to Caesar and was a promoter of the Imperial Cult – probably refers to *"Satan's Seat"* in verse 13.
2. Temple to Zeus and Aphrodite
3. Temple dedicated to Aesculapius – *"God of Healing"* (Insignia was the entwined serpent on the staff. This is still a medical symbol today.)[26]

B. <u>The Persistence of the Church</u> – verse 13
*Many had been persistent in their faith.

"Holdest fast my name"

"Hast not denied my faith"

*We must remain persistent and steadfast in an evil and unchristian world.

"Therefore, my beloved brethren, be ye steadfast, unmoveable, always abounding in the work of the Lord, forasmuch as ye know that your labour is not in vain in the Lord." **1 Corinthians 15:58 KJV**

*These Christians took a stand for God.

*One of the faithful martyrs is mentioned – Antipas.

*Nothing is known of Antipas except that he died for his faith and stand in the Lord Jesus

II. THE CONFLICT – verse 13
"Satan's Seat Is"

"Satan Dwelleth"
*A reference to Roman emperor worship or perhaps of the
  worship of Zeus or both.
*This reveals to us the conflict between the church of God and
  the enemy of God which is Satan.
*It is a reminder of spiritual warfare.
*Satan has declared war on the church.
*The Lord's church is under attack.
"Be sober, be vigilant; because your adversary the devil as a
  roaring lion, walketh about, seeking whom he may devour."
1 Peter 5:8 KJV
*In the face of persecution and tribulation the church of the
  Lord Jesus Christ keeps marching on!

III. THE COMPROMISE – verses 14 and 15
*They had compromised with evil.
*They had a lack of judgment and confrontation for two
  different groups in the church that were promoting false
  doctrine.

A. <u>Doctrine of Balaam</u> – Numbers 22-25, 31
*Balaam had the gift of prophecy, but he had a corrupted
  heart because of money.
*Balak, King of Moab, offered Balaam a sizeable payment
  to curse Israel. The Lord restrained him and all Balaam
  could do was bless the people.
*When he could not curse them, he corrupted them.
*The Moabite girls seduced the men of Israel by inviting
  them to participate in their idolatrous and immoral feasts.
*Through these unholy, unequally yoked marriages, 24,000
  fell in Israel.
*Israel compromised with the world – mixed marriages,
  fornication, adultery, prostitution, idol worship, etc.
"Love not the world, neither the things that are in the
  world. If any man love the world, the love of the Father is
  not in him." **1 John 2:15 KJV**
". . . whosoever therefore will be a friend of the world is
  the enemy of God." **James 4:4 KJV**

B. <u>Nicolaitans</u> – **verse 15**
  *The Nicolaitans were mentioned concerning the church at Ephesus – verse 6.
  *They were apparently a sect which advocated license in matters of Christian conduct, including free love.
  *A reminder that the church is to remain pure and holy in an unholy society and world.
  "That he might present it to himself a glorious church, not having spot, or wrinkle, or any such thing; but that it should be holy and without blemish."
  Ephesians 5:27 KJV

IV. THE CHOICE – verse 16

  *The church at Pergamos had one of two choices.
  A. <u>Denouncement</u> – *"Repent"* – to denounce sin
  B. <u>Destruction</u>
  *God would destroy them for their lack of purity.
  "I tell you, nay: but except ye repent, ye shall all likewise perish." **Luke 13:3 KJV**

V. THE COMMENDATION – verse 17

  *To the overcomers the Lord promises three things.
  A. <u>To Eat of the Hidden Manna</u> – Satisfaction
    *Manna is heavenly bread – Exodus 16:4, 15
    *Christ is a type of manna – Bread of Life (John 6:32-35)
    *Golden container of manna was kept in the most Holy Place in the tabernacle as a memorial to God's faithfulness (Hebrews 9:4 and Exodus 16:32-34)
  B. <u>White Stone</u> – Acceptance
    *Voting Stone (White Stone) approval or acquittal.
    *Special guests were often given a white stone.
    *We have been accepted by Christ.
    "There is therefore now no condemnation to them which are in Christ Jesus, who walk not after the flesh, but after the spirit." **Romans 8:1 KJV**
  C. <u>A New Name Written</u>
    *Heavenly, holy, righteous name.
    *This new name may refer to the Christian's name or a holy name for Christ to give us insight into his holy character.

"Stand up, stand up for Jesus!
Ye soldiers of the cross;
Lift high His royal banner,
It must not suffer loss:
From vict'ry unto vict'ry,
His army shall He lead,
Till every foe is vanquished,
And Christ is Lord indeed."
George Duffield, Jr.[27]

"THE CHURCH AT THYATIRA"
Revelation 2:18-29

*Thyatira – Though smaller and less significant than the first three cities, it received the longest letter.
1. It was half-way between Pergamos and Sardis
2. City of industrial activity – lots of trade and commerce
3. There were many trade guilds there – organized groups and associations for potters, tanners, bronze workers, and dyers.
4. It was said that the water around Thyatira was so adapted to dyeing that in no other place in the world could the scarlet cloth, out of which fezzes were made, be so permanently and perfectly dyed as there.
5. Lydia – *"A Seller of Purple"* was from Thyatira (Acts 16:14). Many scholars believe that she helped start the church and had a tremendous influence upon it by her testimony and witness. One believer can make a big difference.[28]

I. THE CHARACTER OF JESUS – verse 18
  *We are given insight into the character of Jesus.
  ### A. <u>Son of God</u>
  *Jesus is divine! He is God! He is more than a man.
  "In the beginning was the Word, and the Word was with God, and the Word was God." **John 1:1 KJV**
  "Whosoever shall confess that Jesus is the Son of God, God dwelleth in him; and he in God." **1 John 4:15 KJV**
  ### B. <u>Eyes Like a Flame of Fire</u> – Omniscient Power
  *Christ is all seeing and all knowing – verse 23

"The heart is deceitful above all things, and desperately wicked: who can know it? I the Lord search the heart, I try the reigns, even to give every man according to his ways, and according to the fruit of his doings."
Jeremiah 17:9, 10 KJV

"O Lord, thou hast searched me, and known me. Thou knowest my downsitting and mine uprising, thou understandest my thought afar off. Thou compasseth my path and my lying down, and art acquainted with all my ways. For there is not a word in my tongue, but lo, O Lord, thou knowest it altogether." **Psalm 139:1-4 KJV**

*Christ knows and sees everything.

"But Jesus did not commit himself unto them, because he knew all men, and needed not that any should testify of man: for he knew what was in man." **John 2:24, 25 KJV**

"The eyes of the Lord are in every place, beholding the evil and the good." **Proverbs 15:3 KJV**

C. <u>Feet Like Brass</u> – Symbol of Judgment

*Serpent of Brass – Numbers 21:9

*Sin must be judged.

"Henceforth there is laid up for me a crown of righteousness, which the Lord, the righteous judge, shall give me at that day: and not to me only, but unto all them also that love his appearing." **2 Timothy 4:8 KJV**

*Three things are revealed concerning the character of Christ – **DEITY, OMISCIENCE, AND JUDGMENT.**

II. THE COMPLIMENTS TO THE CHURCH – verse 19

*The Lord compliments the church for five things.

A. <u>Charity or Love</u>

*This was a loving congregation.

*Love should be the banner over every church.

"By this shall all men know that ye are my disciples, if ye have love one to another." **John 13:35 KJV**

B. <u>Service</u> – Ministry

*They were a church that served the Lord in ministry.

"Serve the Lord with gladness."
Psalm 100:2 KJV

19

"For God is not unrighteous to forget your work and labour of love, which ye have shewed toward his name, in that ye have ministered to the saints, and do minister."
Hebrews 6:10 KJV

C. Faith
"But without faith it is impossible to please him . . . ."
Hebrews 11:6 KJV
*The Church of Rome was known for its faith –
Romans 1:8

D. Patience
*They were patient and enduring.
"But let patience have her perfect work, that ye may be perfect and entire, wanting nothing." **James 1:4 KJV**

E. Works
*Works are mentioned twice.
*They were hard workers for the sake of the kingdom.
"For as the body without the spirit is dead, so faith without works is dead also." **James 2:26 KJV**

III. THE COMPLAINT AGAINST THE CHURCH – verse 20
*Great contrast between Thyatira and Ephesus – verse 2:2
*The church at Thyatira had allowed the world to creep into its midst.
"Be ye not unequally yoked together with unbelievers: for what fellowship hath righteousness with unrighteousness? And what communion hath light with darkness?"
2 Corinthians 6:14 KJV
*JEZEBEL – woman in the church who actually may have been named Jezebel or probably was being associated with the wicked Jezebel of 1 Kings 16 and 2 King 9 that Elijah had dealings with.
OLD TESTAMENT JEZEBEL
*Jezebel of the Old Testament was married to Ahab who had set up the worship of Baal in Israel (1 Kings 16:29-33).
*She was a wicked and sinful woman.
*Slew all the prophets of Jehovah on whom she could lay her hands on (1 Kings 18:4-13).

*She secured Naboth's vineyard for Ahab by causing Naboth to be murdered (1 Kings 21).

*She was run over by Jehu's chariot, her blood splattered on the wall, and the dogs ate her body. They left nothing but her skull, feet, and the palms of her hands (2 Kings 9:7, 30-37).

*The influence of this woman Jezebel led to the following in this church.

A. **False Teaching** – verse 20

B. **Immorality** – verse 20

C. **Idolatry** – verse 20

IV. THE CHOICE FOR EVIL DOERS

*God gives two choices to the evil doers.

A. **Repentance** – verses 21, 22

*God is a merciful God.

*He even gave Jezebel an opportunity to repent.

"Let the wicked forsake his way, and the unrighteous man his thoughts: and let him return unto the Lord, and he will have mercy upon him; and to our God, for he will abundantly pardon." **Isaiah 55:7 KJV**

B. **Ruin** – verses 22, 23

*God promises to bring judgment upon those who refuse to repent.

"I tell you, nay: but, except ye repent, ye shall all likewise perish." **Luke 13:3 KJV**

V. THE CONQUERORS REWARDS

*Notice the rewards for those who overcome.

A. **Authority** – verse 27

*This is a reference to the rule of the saints of God over the nations during the Millennial Reign of Christ.

*We will be as priests of God during the Millennium.

"But the saints of the most High shall take the kingdom, and possess the kingdom for ever, even for ever and ever." **Daniel 7:18 KJV**

B. **Unique and Close Relationship with Christ** – verse 28

*Jesus is the Bright and Morning Star – Revelation 22:16

*You are going to get a star!!

*Hollywood Boulevard Walk of Fame

"Serve the Lord with gladness in our works and ways
Come before His presence with our songs of praise
Unto Him our Maker we would pledge anew
Life's supreme devotion to service true.

Serve Him with gladness, enter His courts with song;
To our Creator true praises belong:
Great is His mercy, wonderful is His Name.
We gladly serve Him, His great love proclaim."
B. B. McKinney[29]

"THE CHURCH AT SARDIS"
Revelation 3:1-6

Sardis

*The greatest compliment that can be given to a church is for
someone to say "that church is alive!"
*The worst things that can be said about a church is for someone to
say "that church is dead!"
*A dead church has no ministry, no revival, no outreach, no vision,
etc.
*The church at Sardis was a **DEAD** church.

I. THE CHURCH – verse 1
A. <u>The Place</u> – verse 1 – *"Sardis"*
*Ancient capital of Lydia.
*50 miles east of Ephesus.
*It was the junction of five major roads.
*It was an important trade center.
*It was also a military base. It was located on an almost
inaccessible plateau.
*Famous for arts and crafts.
*Was the first place to mint gold and silver coinage.
*Known for its manufacture of woolen garments.
*There seems to be from these verses no doctrinal problems
or opposition or persecution within or against the church.[30]
B. <u>The Person</u> – verse 1
1. *"These thing saith he that hath the seven spirits"*

".. . grace be unto you, and peace, from him which is,
and which was, and which is to come; and from the
seven spirits which are before his throne."

Revelation 1:4 KJV

*Reference to the fullness of the Holy Spirit and His
ministry.

"Seven" = complete, entire, fullness

*The Holy Spirit is the source of life. He produces life in
the church.

2. *"The Seven Stars"*

*Refers to the messengers or pastors.

*Christ is the total authority and head of the church.

*The pastor is not the head, but the under shepherd.

".. . Christ is the head of the church: and he is
the Savior of the Body." **Ephesians 5:23 KJV**

*In order for a church to be alive the Holy Spirit must
be present, and Christ must be the head!

C. <u>The Problem</u> – **verse 1** – *"thou hast a name that thou livest
and art dead"*

*They were a spiritually dead church.

*They had religious ritualism and formalism but no life.

*On the outside they seemed to be alive – in "Name" only.

*Their reputation was one of growth and living.

*The unsaved in Sardis saw the church as a respectable
group of people who were neither dangerous not desirable.

*They were like **ARTIFICIAL FLOWERS.**

*Artificial flowers are beautiful, but not real.

"Wherefore the Lord said, forasmuch as this people draw
near me with their mouth, and with their lips do honor me,
but have removed their heart far from me."

Isaiah 29:13 KJV

*They were simply going through the motions.

*The basic problem was a loss of vision.

*They had lost their vision for God.

"Where there is no vision, the people perish."

Proverbs 29:18 KJV

*We must never lose our vision for the lost and the purpose
of the church.

*The purpose of the church is threefold.
1. To Evangelize Sinners
2. To Edify Saints
3. To Exalt the Savior

II. THE COMMANDS – verses 2, 3
A. <u>*Be Watchful*</u> – verse 2
"Watchful" – idea of being wakeful and alert
*What are we watching for?
*The Coming of Christ – verse 3
"Watch therefore: for ye know neither the day nor the hour wherein the Son of man cometh." **Matthew 25:13 KJV**
*The Lord will come as a thief – verse 3.
*Reference to the rapture – quietly and secretively
"Behold, I come as a thief. Blessed is he that watcheth."
Revelation 16:15 KJV
"For yourselves know perfectly that the day of the Lord so cometh as a thief in the night . . . . But ye, brethren, are not in darkness, that that day should overtake you as a thief." **1 Thessalonians 5:2, 4 KJV**
*A watchful church will be a living and dynamic church.
B. <u>*Strengthen the Things which Remain*</u> – verse 2
*Strengthen the good things which remain.
*Revival and Renewal.
*Focus on your strengths.
*Take hold of every opportunity for improvement.
*Adjust your priorities. Get back to the basics.
C. <u>*Remember, Hold Fast, and Repent*</u> – verse 3
*Similar to verse 2:5 (Ephesus)
*Remembrance and reflection are good things.
*Key word is *"repent."*
*Turn back to God!
"I tell you, Nay: but except ye repent, ye shall all likewise perish." **Luke 13:3 KJV**
"If my people, which are called by my name, shall humble themselves, and pray, and seek my face, and turn from their wicked ways; then will I hear from heaven, and will forgive their sin, and will heal their land."
2 Chronicles 7:14 KJV

III. THE COMMITTED – verse 4

A. <u>Their Faithfulness</u>

*There was a small group in this church that had remained faithful.

*There are always a faithful few who are the glue that holds things together within the church.

*God always has a remnant!

*Israel always had a remnant of faithful people.

*Those who had not defiled their garments were in the minority, not many in number.

*If you are truly committed to Christ, you will be in the minority.

"Enter ye in at the strait gate: for wide is the gate, and broad is the way, that leadeth to destruction, and many there be which go in thereat: because strait is the gate, and narrow is the way, which leadeth unto life, and few there be that find it." **Matthew 7:13-14 KJV**

B. <u>Their Attire</u> – *"White Garments"*

*They had on the proper attire and dress.

*There is a certain etiquette about dress in the military.

*Christians must exercise care about the wardrobe of the soul.

*We are to take off the old man and put on the new man – Colossians 3:8-14.

IV. COMMENDATION – verse 5

A. <u>Pardon</u> – *"White Garments"*

B. <u>Eternal Security</u> – *"I will not blot his name out of the book of life"*

C. <u>Recognition</u> – *"Confess his name before my Father and before his angels"*

"Coming now to Thee, O Christ my Lord,
Trusting only in Thy precious word,
Let my humble pray'r to Thee be heard,
And send a great revival in my soul.

Send a great revival in my soul,
Send a great revival in my soul;

Let the Holy Spirit come and take control,
And send a great revival in my soul."
B. B. McKinney[31]

"THE CHURCH AT PHILADELPHIA"
Revelation 3:7-13
*Note the following:

I. THE ASSEMBLY – verse 7
   *Nothing negative is said about the church.
   *Located 30 miles southeast of Sardis.
   *Located on a strategic place on the main route of the imperial
   post from Rome to the east, and thus was called *"The Gateway
   to the East."*
   *Also, called *"Little Athens"* because of the many temples in
   the city.[32]
   *Chief deity was Dionysus – God of wine.
   *Philadelphia sat on a geological fault. It was prone to
   earthquakes. The city was destroyed in 17 B. C. by an
   earthquake and was rebuilt.
   *Philadelphia means *"Brotherly Love"*[33]
   *Throughout the Scriptures we are told to have love for one
   another.
   "But as touching brotherly love ye need not that I write unto
   you: for ye yourselves are taught by God to love one another."
   1 Thessalonians 4:9 KJV
   "A new commandment I give unto you, that ye love one another;
   as I have loved you, that ye also love one another. By this shall
   all men know that ye are my disciples, if ye have love one to
   another." **John 13:34, 35 KJV**
   "Beloved, let us love one another: for love is of God; and
   everyone that loveth is born of God, and knoweth God."
   1 John 4:7 KJV
   "We know that we have passed from death unto life, because we
   love the brethren . . . ." **1 John 3:14 KJV**

26

II. THE AUTHOR – verse 7

*The risen Lord presents Himself to each of these churches in a different way and always in keeping with the need of each individual church.

A. The Holiness of Christ – verse 7 *"He that is Holy"*

*Christ is holy. Holiness is an essential attribute of the deity of the Lord Jesus.

"For such an high priest became us, who is holy, harmless, undefiled, separate from sinners, made higher than the heavens." **Hebrews 7:26 KJV**

"Who did no sin, neither was guile found in his mouth."
1 Peter 2:22 KJV

*Jesus Christ is sinless and perfect.

"And ye know that he was manifested to take away our sins; and in him is no sin." **1 John 3:5 KJV**

*Because he is perfect in WHO he is, he is also perfect in WHAT he does.

B. Truth of Christ – *"He that is true"*

*Jesus is the true one! Genuine and not a copy.

"As the 'Holy One,' Christ is right in character; as the 'true one,' he is right in conduct."
G. Campbell Morgan[34]

"Jesus saith unto him, I am the way, the truth, and the life: no man cometh unto the Father, but by me."
John 14:6 KJV

"And we know that the Son of God is come, and hath given us an understanding, that we may know him that is true, and we are in him that is true, even in his Son Jesus Christ. This is the true God, and eternal life." **1 John 5:20 KJV**

C. The Authority of Christ – verse 7 –
"Key of David, he that openeth"

*This reveals the authority of Christ.

*The whole book of Revelation reveals His unique authority.

"I am he that liveth, and was dead; and behold, I am alive for evermore, Amen; and have the keys of hell and of death."
Revelation 1:18 KJV

*Jesus is greater than David (King of Israel)

"For unto us a child is born, unto us a son is given: and the government shall be upon his shoulder: and his name shall be called wonderful, counsellor, the mighty God, the everlasting father, the prince of peace. Of the increase of his government and peace there shall be no end, upon the throne of David, and upon his kingdom, to order it, and to establish it with judgement and with justice from henceforth even for ever." **Isaiah 9:6, 7 KJV**

"He shall be great, and shall be called the Son of the Highest: and the Lord God shall give unto him the throne of his father David: and he shall reign over the house of Jacob forever; and of his kingdom there shall be no end."

Luke 1:32, 33 KJV

*Because of His authority, Jesus opened a great door of SERVICE for them – verses 7, 8

III. THE APPROVAL – verse 8

*The Lord commends them for three major things.

A. Strength – *"Thou hast a little strength"*

*God is the source of strength.

"I can do all things through Christ which strengtheneth me." **Philippians 4:13 KJV**

"But they that wait upon the Lord shall renew their strength; they shall mount up with wings as eagles; they shall run, and not be weary; and they shall walk, and not faint." **Isaiah 40:31 KJV**

B. Faithfulness – *"Thou hast kept my Word"*

*They had been faithful to the Word of God!

"Moreover it is required in stewards, that a man be found faithful." **1 Corinthians 4:2 KJV**

C. Courage – *"Thou hast not denied my name"*

*They had taken a stand against the enemies of Christ and His church.

"Have not I commanded thee? Be strong and of a good courage; be not afraid, neither be thou dismayed; for the Lord thy God is with thee whitersoever thou goest."

Joshua 1:8 KJV

IV. **THE ASSURANCE** – verse 10
  *The Lord assures the church that they will be protected from the Great Tribulation.
  *Don't fear the End Time Events!!

V. **THE APPEAL** – verse 11
  *Christ reminds them that he is coming again.
  *The Second Coming is a fact and a certainty.
  *The appeal is for them to keep up the good work.
  "Hold fast that which thou hast"
  *Be careful of your crown.
  *Church at Smyrna!!
  ". . . Be thou faithful unto death, and I will give thee a crown of life." **Revelation 2:10 KJV**

VI. **THE ACCOLADES** – Recognition of Merit
  A. <u>Earthly Recognition</u> – verse 9
    *The false members of the synagogue of Satan would be judged and truly know that the church is the TRUE organization of God!
  B. <u>Heavenly Recognition</u> – verse 12
    *Two main ideas:
    1. <u>Establishment</u>
      "Pillar in the Temple of God"
    2. <u>Identification</u>
      "Write" appears at least twice.
      *You write your name on things to identify it as your possession.
      *We are Christ's possession.

"We are one in the bond of love;
We are one in the bond of love.
We have joined our spirit with the Spirit of God;
We are one in the bond of love."
Otis Skillings[35]

"THE CHURCH AT LAODICEA"
Revelation 3:14-22

*City of Laodicea

1. Founded by Antiochus II and named after his wife.[36]
2. There were three major highways that ran through the city of Laodicea.
3. Highly successful commercial and financial center.
4. City of wealthy bankers, businessmen, and financiers – Highly socialized.
5. "The many millionaires combined to build theaters, a huge stadium, lavish public baths, and fabulous shopping centers." **Lehman Strauss**[37]
6. Great medical center and school located there.
7. Manufacture of a special eye salve and other medicines – **verse 18.**
8. Also known for a glossy black wool cloth produced there – carpets and cloaks were made from this wool.
9. They obtained their pure, cold drinking water from the city of Colossae.
10. Nearby were famous hot springs.[38]
11. Nothing good is said about the church in this passage.
12. They were a church that had forgotten their purpose, mission, and vision.

I. THE POSITION OF CHRIST

*Jesus reveals His unique and exalted position.

*In order for a church to be effective it must realize the proper position of the Lord Jesus Christ.

*A church is blessed by God when Jesus Christ is preeminent.

A. <u>The Immortality of Christ</u> – verse 14 – "*Amen*"

"*Amen*" translates "truth" both in Hebrew and Greek.[39]

*Reveals His Sovereignty and Supremacy

*We often say "Amen!" after a great statement as an indication of approval.

*We also close our prayers by saying "AMEN!"

*Christ is the Final Word.

*He is the best. There is no improving upon Him.

"Now unto the King eternal, immortal, invisible, the only wise God, be honour and glory for ever and ever. Amen."
1 Timothy 1:17 KJV

B. **The Integrity of Christ** – verse 4
"Faithful and True Witness"
*Mentioned in Revelation 1:5.
*Jesus is the real thing. Dependable.
*You can count on Christ and His testimony as the faithful and true witness of the Lord Jesus Christ.
"I am the way, the truth, and the life." **John 14:6 KJV**

C. **The Influence of Christ** – verse 14
"Beginning of the creation of God"
*Jesus is both the CREATOR of the Universe and the SUSTAINER of the Universe.
*Without Jesus there would be chaos and confusion in this universe.
*Jesus holds it all together.
*This phrase does not mean that Christ was the first of God's created beings, but rather the one in whom creation had its beginning.
"And all things were made by him; and without him was not anything made that was made." **John 1:3 KJV**
"For by him were all things created, that are in heaven, and that are in earth, visible and invisible, whether they be thrones, or dominions, or principalities, or powers: all things were created by him, and for him."
Colossians 1:16 KJV

D. **The Intelligence of Christ** – verse 15 - *"I know thy works"*
*Jesus knows everything about us.
*He is omniscient – "all knowing"
"O Lord, thou hast searched me, and known me. Thou knowest my downsitting and mine uprising, thou understandest my thought afar off."
Psalm 139:2 KJV
*The fact that Jesus knows everything about you should comfort you and challenge you.

II. THE PROBLEM OF THE CHURCH
*They were *"lukewarm"* – neither hot or cold.

*Churches are filled with lukewarm Christians.
*Lukewarmness makes God sick – verse 16.
*Lukewarmness is repulsive, sickening, disgusting.
*God would rather you be hot or cold.
*Their lukewarmness was a result of three things.

A. **Self-Righteousness** – **verse 17**
"Have need of nothing"
    *They were filled with pride and arrogance.
    "Pride goeth before destruction, and an haughty
      spirit before a fall." **Proverbs 16:18 KJV**
    *They were self-righteous in their buildings, budgets, and
      programs.

B. **Sightlessness** – **verse 17** – *"Blind"*
    *Could not see their condition.
    *Pharisees were blinded also – John 9:39-41
    *Satan and sin blind.
    "In whom the God of this world hath blinded the minds of
      them which believe not, lest the light of the glorious
      gospel of Christ, who is the image of God, should shine
      unto them." **2 Corinthians 4:4 KJV**

C. **Shamefulness** – **verse 17** – *"naked"*
    *Their shame is mentioned in verse 18.
    *They were rich materially, but poor spiritually.
    *They had wealth, but not works.
    *They were not doing much for the sake of the
      Kingdom of God.
    "Wretched" – Distress
    "Miserable" – Pitiful
    "Poor"
    "Naked" – No works to clothe them

III. **THE PRESCRIPTION FOR A CURE**
    *Jesus outlines what they need to do as a church.
    *Three steps to renewal and restoration!!

A. **Realization** – **verse 18**
    *Christ counsels them to examine themselves.
    "But let a man examine himself."
                    1 Corinthians 11:28 KJV
    "Buy of me gold tried in the fire" –

32

Righteousness of Christ
"White Raiment" – White – Purity
Pardon of God and His Righteousness
"Anoint thine eyes with eye salve"
*Christ is the ultimate eye doctor
*His light shines in the darkness.
B. Repentance – verse 19
    *Repent of your sin and turn to the Lord Jesus Christ.
    *Repent means to confess and forsake.
    "I tell you, Nay: but except ye repent, ye shall all likewise perish." **Luke 13:3 KJV**
C. Reception – verse 20 – *"Sup"* – Fellowship
    *In order to be in a right relationship with God, you must renew your fellowship and communion with the Savior.
    *Christ pleads with you to let him come in.
    *Christ does three things.
1. Stands – Christ is standing to come in
2. Knocks – Christ is knocking to come in
3. Speaks – Christ is asking to come in
*Will you allow Jesus to come into your life.

"The Savior is waiting to enter your heart,
Why don't you let Him come in?
There's nothing in this world to keep you apart,
What is your answer to Him?

Time, after time, He has waited before,
And now He is waiting again
To see if you're willing to open the door,
Oh, how He wants to come in."
Ralph Carmichael[40]

"THE RAPTURE"
Revelation 4:1

*The Bible refers to two distinct comings of the Lord Jesus Christ.
1. The Rapture – Revelation 4:1

A. Jesus comes as a *"Thief in the Night"* – 1 Thessalonians 5:2

B. Jesus will return in the air – 1 Thessalonians 4:17

2. The Glorious Return (Second Coming) – Revelation 19:11

A. *"Every eye shall behold Him"* – Revelation 1:7

B. Jesus will actually touch down on the earth – Revelation 19:11-16

   *Zechariah 14:4 – *"Feet shall stand on the Mount of Olives"*

"Rapture" – Comes from the phrase, *"caught up"* in 1 Thessalonians 4:17

Greek word, *"harpazo,"* means "to seize" or "to snatch up."

"Rapti" – Archaic, Latin word that means a catching away, to be caught up, to be snatched away, to carry off. Used in the Latin Vulgate.[41]

*Dr. Kenneth S. Wuest – Greek Scholar and Theologian, gives the following meanings of the word.

1. To Catch Away Speedily – Acts 8:39 – The Spirit *"caught away"* Philip after he led the Ethiopian Eunuch to Christ.
2. To Seize by Force
3. To Claim for One's Own Self
4. To Move to a New Place
5. To Rescue from Danger[42]

I. THE CERTAINTY OF THE RAPTURE

*The rapture (return of the Lord Jesus Christ) is a promised event.

*It will be literal and personal.

A. It is Promised in the Old Testament

"I saw in the night visions, and behold, one like the Son of man came with the clouds of heaven." **Daniel 7:13 KJV**

B. It is Promised by Jesus

"And if I go and prepare a place for you, I will come again, and receive you unto myself; that where I am, there ye may be also." **John 14:3 KJV**

C. It is Proclaimed by the Angels

*At the Ascension on the Mount of Olives

"And while they looked steadfastly toward heaven as he
went up, behold, two men stood by them in white apparel;
Which also said, Ye men of Galilee, why stand ye gazing
up into heaven? This same Jesus, which is taken up from
you into heaven, shall so come in like manner as ye have
seen him go into heaven." **Acts 1:10, 11 KJV**

D. It is Predicted by the New Testament Writers

1. Apostle Paul

"Looking for that blessed hope, and the glorious
appearing of the great God and our Savior Jesus Christ."
Titus 2:13 KJV

2. Apostle James

"Be ye also patient: stablished your hearts: for the
coming of the Lord draweth nigh." **James 5:8 KJV**

3. Apostle Peter

"And when the chief Shepherd shall appear, ye shall
receive a crown of glory that fadeth not away."
1 Peter 5:4 KJV

4. Apostle John

"Beloved, now are we the sons of God, and it doth not yet
appear what we shall be: but we know that, when he
shall appear we shall be like him; for we shall see him
as he is." **1 John 3:3 KJV**

II. THE CHARACTERISTICS OF THE RAPTURE

*The 1 Thessalonians 4:16-18 reveals several characteristics of
the rapture.

"For the Lord himself shall descend with a shout, with the
voice of the archangel, and with the trump of God: and the
dead in Christ shall rise first: Then we which are alive and
remain shall be caught up together with them in the clouds, to
meet the Lord in the air: and so shall we ever be with the
Lord. Wherefore comfort one another with these words."
1 Thessalonians 4:16-18 KJV

A. The Sounds of His Coming

*Three sounds are revealed. They are interrelated.

1. *"Shout"* – Military command to call for believers to
come home! Shout of attention!

2. *"Voice of the Archangel"* – Voice of organization and instruction. Also, to herald Christ's coming.
3. *"Trumpet of God"* – to summons the dead to come forth out of the grave – 1 Thessalonians 4:16

B. The Sequence of His Coming
*The dead shall rise first.
*Then the *"alive"* will be caught up!
*It will occur instantaneously.

C. The Secretiveness of His Coming
*It is described as a *"thief in the night"* – 1 Thessalonians 5:2
*No one knows when Jesus is going to return.
"But of that day and hour knoweth no man, no not the angels of heaven, but my Father only."
Matthew 24:36 KJV

D. The Suddenness of His Coming
*It will happen suddenly – 1 Thessalonians 5:3
"Sudden Destruction"
"For as lightning cometh out of the east, and shineth even unto the west; so shall also the coming of the Son of man be." **Matthew 24:27 KJV**
"In the Twinkling of an eye" – slightest movement of the eyeball - 1 Corinthians 15:52

III. THE CONSEQUENCES OF THE RAPTURE
"Then shall two be in the field; the one shall be taken, and the other left. Two women shall be grinding at the mill; the one shall be taken, and the other left."
Matthew 24:40, 41 KJV

A. There will be Separation
B. There will be Sorrow
C. There will be Shamefulness
*Parable of the Ten Virgins – Matthew 25:1-13 (Embarrassment)
*Unprepared and left behind.
D. There will be Suffering (Great Tribulation)

IV. THE CHALLENGE OF THE RAPTURE

*The challenge of the rapture is to be ready when it occurs.
"Therefore be ye also ready: for in such an hour as ye think not the Son of man cometh." **Matthew 24:44 KJV**

A. We Should Look for Jesus

*We should be watchful for His arrival.
"Looking for that blessed hope, and glorious appearing of the great God and our Savior Jesus Christ."
Titus 2:13 KJV
"Watch therefore, for ye know neither the day nor the hour wherein the Son of man cometh." **Matthew 24:13 KJV**

*"The sky shall unfold-preparing His entrance
The stars shall applaud Him-with thunder of praise.
The sweet light in His eyes shall enhance those awaiting
And we shall behold him-then face to face."*
Dottie Rambo[43]

B. We Should Labor for Jesus

*We should serve the Lord.
"Therefore, my beloved brethren, be ye steadfast, unmoveable, always abounding in the work of the Lord, forasmuch as ye know that your labor is not in vain in the Lord." **1 Corinthians 15:58 KJV**

*"We'll work till Jesus Comes,
We'll work till Jesus Comes,
We'll work till Jesus Come,
And we'll be gathered home."*
Elizabeth Mills[44]

C. We Should Live for Jesus

"Teaching us that, denying ungodliness and worldly lusts, we should live soberly, righteously, and godly, in this present world." **Titus 2:12 KJV**

"And now, little children, abide in him: that, when he shall appear, we may have confidence, and not be ashamed before him at his coming. If ye know that he is righteous, ye know that every one that doeth righteousness is born of him." **1 John 2:28, 30 KJV**

"Some golden day-break Jesus will come;
Some golden day-break, battles all won,
He'll shout the victory, break thro' the blue,
Some golden day-break, for me, for you."
Carl A. Blackmore[45]

"THE GREAT TRIBULATION PERIOD"
(Overview)
Revelation 4:1 and Revelation 19:11

*Immediately after the Rapture of the church, there will be a period of time known as the *"Great Tribulation"* that will take place on the earth.

*The term, *"Great Tribulation,"* comes from Revelation 7:14.

*John MacArthur, Jr. defines the Tribulation Period as follows:

The Tribulation refers to that seven-year time period immediately following the Rapture-removal of the church from the earth (John 14:1-3; 1 Thess. 4:13-18), when the righteous judgments of God will be poured out upon an unbelieving world (Jer. 30:7; Dan. 9:27; 12:1; 2 Thess. 2:7-12; Rev. 16). These judgments will be climaxed by the return of Christ in glory to the earth (Matt. 24:27-31; 25:31-46; 2 Thess.2:7-12).[46]

*This period of time is described and explained in the book of Revelation (Revelation 4:1-19:11).

*There are several key aspects of the Tribulation Period that are important to consider.

I. THE UNDENIABLE CERTAINTY OF THE TRIBULATION PERIOD

*The Tribulation Period will take place immediately after the

38

Rapture.

"And at that time shall Michael stand up, the great prince which standeth for the children of thy people: and there shall be a time of trouble, such as never since there was a nation, even to that same time: and at that time thy people shall be delivered, every one that shall be found written in the book."

Daniel 12:1 KJV

A. The Duration of the Tribulation Period

*The total duration of the Tribulation Period is seven years.

*The Tribulation Period is the 70th week of Daniel which is mentioned in Daniel 9:27.

*The latter half of the Tribulation Period will be terrible and is said to be 42 months or 1,260 days (Revelation 11:2, 3; 12:6).

B. The Description of the Tribulation Period

*The Tribulation Period will be a time of unprecedented natural phenomenon and divine judgment.

"For then shall be great tribulation, such as was not since the beginning of the world to this time, no, nor ever shall be."

Matthew 24:21 KJV

1. It will be a Time of CHAOS

*The Tribulation Period will be marked by great confusion and chaos when Jesus raptures Christians out of this world.

"Then shall two be in the field; the one shall be taken, and the other left. Two women shall be grinding at the mill; the one shall be taken, and the other left."

Matthew 24:40, 41 KJV

2. It will be a Time of CONDEMNATION

*See Revelation 6:16, 17

3. It will be a Time of CONFLICT (War)

*See Revelation 6:3, 4; Revelation 12:17

4. It will be a Time of CARNAGE (Death)

*See Revelation 6:7, 8; Revelation 16:3

5. It will be a Time of CALAMITY

*See Revelation 8:7

6. It will be a Time of CONTAMINATION

*See Revelation 8:10, 11

7. *It will be a Time of CATASTROPHE*
*See Revelation 8:12, 13

II. THE UNIQUE CHARACTERISTICS OF THE TRIBULATION PERIOD
A. The Antichrist will Rise to Power and Rule the World
"Little Children, it is the last time: and as ye have heard that antichrist shall come." **1 John 2:18 KJV**
*The Antichrist will rise to power immediately after the rapture of the church (Revelation 6:1, 2).
B. The Tribulation Period is God's Last Dealings with the Jews, His Chosen People
*God is not finished with the Jews!
*Read Daniel 9:24.
"Alas! For that day is great, so that none is like it: it is even time of Jacob's trouble; but he shall be saved out of it." **Jeremiah 30:7 KJV**
*A Jewish remnant will be saved out of the Tribulation Period (Revelation 7).
C. God's Judgment and Wrath will be Unleashed Upon the Earth
*Read Isaiah 13:6-11
*God will pour out His wrath upon the earth for man's rejection of Jesus Christ as the true Messiah (Isaiah 26:21), the reception of Antichrist (Revelation 14:9, 10), and the persecution of the Jews (Joel 3).
*There are three groups of judgments described in the book of Revelation.
1. *The SEAL Judgments* (Revelation 6)
   A. Antichrist (Revelation 6:1, 2)
   B. War (Revelation 6:3, 4)
   C. Famine (Revelation 6:5, 6)
   D. Death (Revelation 6:7, 8)
   E. Martyrdom (Revelation 6:9-11)
   F. Global Destruction (Revelation 6:12-17)
2. *The TRUMPET Judgments*
   (Revelation 8:7-9:21; 11:15-19)
   A. One-Third of Vegetation Destroyed
      (Revelation 8:7)

B. One-Third of Sea Life and Ships Destroyed
       (Revelation 8:8, 9)
   C. One-Third of the Fresh Water Poisoned
       (Revelation 8:10, 11)
   D. One-Third of the Sun, Moon, and Stars are
       Darkened (Revelation 8:12, 13)
   E. Terrible Locusts that Torment Mankind
       (Revelation 9:1-12)
   F. One-Third of Mankind Killed by Wicked Demonic
       Beings (Revelation 9:13-21)
3. *The VIAL/BOWL Judgments*
   (Revelation 16)
   A. Ugly and Terrible Sores on Those who have the
       Mark of the Beast (Revelation 16:2)
   B. Death of All Sea Life (Revelation 16:3)
   C. Fresh Water Contaminated with Blood
       (Revelation 16:4-7)
   D. Mankind Scorched with Unbearable Heat
       (Revelation 16:8, 9)
   E. Darkness and Pain (Revelation 16:10, 11)
   F. Euphrates River Dries Up to Prepare for Armageddon
       and Vile, Demonic Forces are Unleashed
       (Revelation 16:12-16)
   G. Devasting Earthquake and Hail
       (Revelation 16:17-21)
*Summary of these judgments.
 1. They will be Swift
 2. They will be Severe
 3. They will be Supernatural
 4. They will be Scary

III. THE URGENT COMMAND TO AVOID THE
     TRIBULATION PERIOD
     "Therefore be ye also ready; for in such an hour as ye think not
     the Son of man cometh." **Matthew 24:44 KJV**
     *One can prepare for the coming of Christ in two ways.
   A. <u>Salvation</u>
      "For whosoever shall call upon the name of the Lord shall
      be saved." **Romans 10:13 KJV**

B. Separation

"Teaching us that, denying ungodliness and worldly lusts,
we should live soberly, righteously, and godly, in this
present world." **Titus 2:12 KJV**

"Faithful and true would He find us here
If He should come today?
Watching in gladness and not in fear,
If He should come today?
Signs of His coming multiply,
Morning light breaks in eastern sky,
Watch, for the time is drawing nigh,
What if it were today?"
Leila Naylor Morris[47]

"THE THRONE OF GOD"
Revelation 4:1-11

*In chapter four we enter the section of *"the things which shall be
hereafter"* – **Revelation 1:8**
*The Rapture has taken place and the Church Age is completed –
Revelation 4:1.
*Note the following.

I. The ALMIGHTY – verses 2, 3

A. The Deity of God – verse 2

*The One on the throne is Almighty God.

*The *"throne"* represents the deity and sovereignty of God.

"Before the mountains were brought forth, or ever thou
hadst formed the earth, and the world, even from
everlasting to everlasting, thou art God."
Psalm 90:2 KJV

"I am the Lord, and there is none else, there is no God
beside me . . . . ." **Isaiah 45:5 KJV**

B. The Beauty of God – verse 2, 3

*God is beautiful.

"One thing have I desired of the Lord, that will I seek after; that I may dwell in the house of the Lord all the days of my life, to behold the beauty of the Lord, and to enquire in his temple." **Psalm 27:4 KJV**

*Four colors are mentioned.

1. *"Jasper"* – verse 3 – Reddish Yellow
2. *"Sardius"* – verse 3 – Blood Red
3. *"Emerald"* – verse 3 – Light Green
4. *"Crystal"* – verse 6 – Clear – *"Sea of Glass"*

*Rainbow around the throne.

*Ezekiel also saw this throne (Ezekiel 1:26-28).

*The rainbow is a symbol of the **FAITHFULNESS** of God as demonstrated in God's promise to Noah (Genesis 9:11-16).

C. <u>The Authority of God</u> – verse 5

  "Lightening, thunders, and voices"

  *God is seated on His throne to execute judgment.

  "And he judges the world with righteousness; he judges the peoples with uprightness." **Psalm 9:8 ESV**

  *In Revelation 20:11-15 He is seated on the throne to judge the lost.

  *In Exodus there is a similar picture on Mount Sinai.

  "And it came to pass on the third day in the morning, that there were thunders and lightnings, and a thick cloud upon the mount, and the voice of the trumpet exceeding loud; so that all the people that was in the camp trembled." **Exodus 19:16 KJV**

D. <u>The Unity of God</u> – verse 5

  "Seven Spirits of God" – Ultimate unity and completion.

  *God is in perfect unity with the **TRINITY.**

  "For there are three that bear witness in heaven: the Father, the Word, and the Holy Spirit: and these three are one."
  1 John 5:7 NKJV

II. **The ASSEMBLY**

  *Note the assembly and host around the throne of God.

  A. <u>Twenty-four Elders</u> – verse 4

    *The 24 Elders are symbolic of the redeemed of mankind.

    *24 refers to the 12 Patriarchs of the Old Testament and the

12 Apostles of the New Testament.
*Note their description.
   1. *"Seated Upon a Throne"* – **verse 4**
       *We will reign with Christ.
       "And hath made us kings and priests unto God and his
       Father . . . ." **Revelation 1:6 KJV**
   2. *"Clothed in White Raiment"* – **verse 4**
       *Christ has washed our sins away.
       "Unto him that loved us, and washed us from our sins
       in his own blood." **Revelation 1:5 KJV**
   3. *"Crowns of Gold"* – **verse 5**
       *Represents the Believers rewards.
       "And when the chief Shepherd shall appear, ye shall
       receive a crown of glory that fadeth not away."
                   2 Peter 5:4 KJV
B. <u>Four Beasts</u> – **verses 6-8**
   *Created angelic beings who praise God continually.
   *Each Beast had a different appearance.
      1. Lion - King
      2. Calf (Young Ox) – Beast of Burden/Service
      3. Man – Highest Intelligence
      4. Eagle – Swiftness, Sovereignty
   "Some students see in the four faces described (Rev. 4:7) an
   illustration of the fourfold picture of Christ given in the
   Gospel accounts. Matthew is the royal Gospel of the King,
   illustrated by the lion. Mark emphasizes the servant aspect
   of the Lord's ministry (the calf). Luke presents Christ
   as the compassionate Son of man. John magnifies the
   deity of Christ, the Son of God (the eagle)."
                   Warren W. Wiersbe[48]

III. **The ADORATION** – **verses 9-11**
   *The twenty-four elders and the four beasts constantly worship
     God.
   *Their worship involved *"glory, honor, and thanks."*
   *They worshipped God for His . . .
   A. <u>Person</u> – **verse 10** - *"Him"*
   B. <u>Position</u> – **verse 10** - *"Sat on the throne"*
   C. <u>Permanence</u> – **verse 10** - *"Liveth forever"*

44

D. Power – verse 11 – *"Created all things"*

*We are to be worshippers of God.

"O worship the Lord in the beauty of holiness: fear
before him, all the earth." **Psalm 96:9 KJV**

"Praise God, from whom all blessings flow;
Praise Him, all creatures here below;
Praise Him above, ye heavenly host;
Praise Father, Son, and Holy Ghost. Amen"
Thomas Ken[49]

"WORTHY OF WORSHIP"
Revelation 5:1-14

*Worship is a major theme throughout the book of Revelation.

*See Revelation 4:10, 11; 5:11-14; 7:11, 12; 11:15, 16; etc.

*Worship is one of the great privileges of the Christian life.

"The call to worship is universal and eternal. It is the call to all
people in every tribe, nation, and generation. It is the highest call
which can be made to an individual. It is the call of God to each of
us, and as true worshipers, we must heed His call."
Sammy Tippit, Worthy of Worship[50]

"Worship" involves reverence, adoration, praise, homage, honor of,
devotion to

*Worship is an . . .

  1. Acclamation of the Mouth – Psalm 150:6, Psalm 29:2

  2. Attitude of the Heart – John 4:26

*Worship is a **SACRIFICE** – Old Testament Sacrifices

"By him therefore let us offer the sacrifice of praise to God
continually, that is, the fruit of our lips giving thanks to his
name." **Hebrews 13:5 KJV**

*Worship is an **ENCOUNTER** with God.

***ISAIAH** had an encounter with God in the Temple - Isaiah 6:1-13

*Note the following in this chapter.

I. THE SEARCH – verses 1-5

A. Reason for the Search – verses 1-3

*A search was made to find someone who could open the
seals of the book/scroll.

45

*What is this book that God the Father is holding?
"The book that John saw in the hand of Him that sat upon
the throne is the title-deed to this world." **H. A. Ironside**[51]
*John MacArthur, Jr., David Jeremiah, John Phillips,
J. Vernon McGee, etc. all concur with this interpretation.
*This interpretation is based upon the titled deed mentioned
in Jeremiah 32:6-15.

B. <u>Reaction to the Search</u> – verse 4
*John wept because no man was worthy to open the
book/scroll.

C. <u>Results of the Search</u> – verse 5
*An announcement is made that Jesus is worthy to open the
seals of the book/scroll.

II. THE SAVIOR – verses 5-8
*Note the following about the Savior.

A. <u>He is the Lion</u> – verse 5
"The image of 'the lion' speaks of dignity, sovereignty,
courage, and victory."
Warren W. Wiersbe[52]
*Jesus was/is from the tribe of Judah.
*Judah is the tribe of David.
*This is the reason that Joseph and Mary had to travel to
Bethlehem for the Roman census.
"And Joseph also went up from Galilee, out of the city of
Nazareth, into Judea, unto the city of David, which is
called Bethlehem; (because he was of the house and
lineage of David." **Luke 2:4 KJV**

B. <u>He is the Lamb</u> - verse 6
*Jesus was/is the sacrificial lamb for the sins of mankind.
". . . Behold the Lamb of God, which taketh away the sin of
the world." **James 1:29 KJV**
"But with the precious blood of Christ, as of a lamb
without blemish and without spot." **1 Peter 1:19 KJV**

III. THE SONG – verses 9-14
*The 24 Elders, the Four Beast, and the host of Heaven sings a
song of worship unto the Lamb.
*They worship Him for His . . .

A. **His Provision** – verse 9
   *Jesus provided the ultimate sacrifice for sin.
   "For when we were yet without strength in due time Christ died for the ungodly." **Romans 5:6 KJV**

B. **His Power** – verses 12, 13
   "All power is given unto me in heaven and in earth."
   Matthew 28:18 KJV

C. **His Position** – verse 13
   *Jesus reigns supreme.
   "He shall be great, and shall be called the Son of the Highest: and the Lord God shall give unto him the throne of his father David: And he shall reign over the house of Jacob forever; and of his kingdom there shall be no end."
   Luke 1:32, 33 KJV

D. **His Permanence** – verses 13, 14
   *Jesus is eternal.
   "Jesus Christ the same yesterday, and today, and forever."
   Hebrews 13:8 KJV

"We will glorify the King of kings,
We will glorify the Lamb;
We will glorify the Lord of lords,
Who is the great I Am."
Twila Paris[53]

"THE SEAL JUDGMENTS OF GOD"
Revelation 6:1-17

*Jesus opens the seals on the Little Book (Revelation 5:1) in this chapter.

*The Great Tribulation begins with the Four Horsemen (Revelation 6:1-8).

*The Tribulation Period is a time of God's Judgment on the earth.
". . . And there shall be a time of trouble, such as never was since there was a nation (Israel) even to that same time."
Daniel 12:1 KJV

*God's Judgement is executed in three series. They are as follows:
1. The Seal Judgements (Revelation 6:1 to 8:5)
2. The Trumpet Judgements – Revelation 8:7-9:21, 11:15-19

47

3. The Vial/Bowl Judgments – Revelation 16
*Note the following:

I. The VIOLENT HORSEMEN – verses 1-8
  *The first four seals are horsemen that bring violence with
  them.
  ### A. The First Seal – (White Horse) – verse 2
  *The White Horse represents **DECEPTION.**
  *David Jeremiah, J. Vernon McGee, Charles Ryrie,
  Lehman, Strauss, etc. agree this rider is the Antichrist.
  (See 1 Thessalonians 5:3 and 2 Thessalonians 2:6-9)
  *"Bow," "Crown," and "White Horse" are symbols of
  power and leadership.
  *He initially deceives the world with peace.
  *This peace will be temporary followed by terror.
  ### B. The Second Seal – (Red Horse) – verses 3, 4
  *The Red Horse represents **DESTRUCTION.**
  "Sword" represents war.
  "Red" represents bloodshed and death.
  ### C. The Third Seal – (Black Horse) – verses 5, 6
  *The Black Horse represents **DEARTH** (Famine).
  *Balances/Scales will be used to measure out the food
  because of the famine.
  *War and famine go together.
  "Our skin was black like an oven because of the terrible
  famine." **Lamentations 5:10 KJV**
  ### D. The Fourth Seal – (Pale Horse) – verses 7, 8
  *The Pale Horse (sickly) represents **DEATH.**
  *Hades follows death.
  *One-fourth of the inhabitants of the world die.
  "Death claims the body while hades claims the soul of the
  dead (Revelation 20:13)." **Warren Wiersbe**[54]

II. The VOICES OF THE MARTYRS – verses 9-11
  *This seal represents individuals who will be saved during the
  Great Tribulation Period, but they will pay with their lives.
  *They will be martyred for their faith.
  *Three things are revealed about them.
  ### A. Their Conversion – verse 9 – "testimony"

B. <u>Their Cry</u> – verse 10 – *"How long, O Lord"*
C. <u>Their Cleansing</u> – verse 11 – *"white robes"*

III. The **VENGEANCE OF GOD** – verses 12-17
*When the sixth seal is opened their will be great cosmic disturbances.
*Three things are revealed in these verses.
A. <u>The Phenomenon</u> – **verses 12-14**
  1. Cataclysmic Earthquake – verse 12
     *There are three earthquakes in Revelation:
       Revelation 6:12; 11:13; and 16:18, 19
  2. Sun becomes black – verse 12
  3. Moon becomes as blood – verse 12
  4. Stars fall from the sky – verse 13
  5. Sky/Atmosphere is altered – verse 14
  6. Land masses are rearranged – verse 14
  "And I will show wonders in the heavens and in the earth,
  blood, and fire, and pillars of smoke. The sun shall be
  turned into darkness, and the moon into blood, before the
  great and terrible day of the Lord come."
            Joel 2:30, 31 KJV
  "Immediately after the tribulation of those days shall the
  sun be darkened, and the moon shall not give her light,
  and the stars shall fall from heaven, and the powers of the
  heavens shall be shaken." **Matthew 24:29 KJV**
B. <u>The Pleas</u> – **verses 15-16**
  *The horror will be so great that men will want to die.
C. <u>The Punishment</u> – **verse 17**
  *God's punishment and wrath are unleased upon the earth.
  "God judgeth the righteous, and God is angry with the
  wicked every day." **Psalm 7:11 KJV**
  "The Lord is known by the judgment which he
  executeth . . . ." **Psalm 9:16**
  "For the wrath of God is revealed from heaven against all
  ungodliness and unrighteousness of men, who hold the
  truth in unrighteousness." **Romans 1:18 KJV**

***Warren W. Wiersbe gives us the following parallel chart of
Matthew 24 and Revelation 6.[55]**

Matthew 24	Revelation 6
False Christs – verses 4, 5	White Horse Rider (Antichrist) – verses 1, 2
Wars – verse 6	Red Horse (war) – verses 3, 4
Famines – verse 7, a	Black Horse (famine) – vss. 5,6
Death – verses 7,b-8	Pale Horse (death) – verses 7, 8
Martyrs – verse 9	Martyrs – verses 9-11
Worldwide Chaos – vss. 10-13	Worldwide Chaos – vss. 12-17

"THE 144,000"
Revelation 7:1-8

*Chapter seven is an interlude and a parenthesis between the sixth seal (Revelation 6:12-17) and the seventh seal (Revelation 8:1).
*The Seventh Seal will be opened in Revelation 8:1.
*Note the following:

I. THE SUSPENSION OF JUDGMENT – verses 1-3
*The suspension of judgment is an act of mercy.
". . . in wrath remember mercy." **Habakkuk 3:2 KJV**
*It allows the world to take a breath.
*Mercy in the midst of Judgment.
 1. Ark – Flood
 2. Blood – Passover in Egypt

II. THE SYMBOLISM OF THE WIND – verse 1
*The *"wind"* is a symbol of the judgment of God.
"And upon Elam will I bring the four winds from the four quarters of heaven, and will scatter them toward all those winds; and there shall be no nation whither the outcasts of Elam shall not come." **Jeremiah 49:36 KJV**
"Thus saith the Lord; Behold, I will raise up against Babylon, and against them that dwell in the midst of them that rise up against me, a destroying wind; And will send unto Babylon fanners, that shall fan her, and shall empty her land: for in the day of trouble they shall be against her round about."
Jeremiah 51:1, 2 KJV

III. THE STRUGGLE OF THE ANGELS – verse 1

*The angels are *"holding back"* the wind.

*The wind is struggling to blow.

*They are standing on the four corners of the earth.

*The four corners of the earth refer to the four points of the compass – north, south, east, and west.

IV. THE SEALING OF THE JEWS – verses 1-8

*The 144,000 are missionaries who will spread the gospel throughout the world.

"These are the ones who are going to witness in the great tribulational period." **J. Vernon McGee**[56]

"And this gospel of the kingdom shall be preached in all the world for a witness unto all nations; and then shall the end come." **Matthew 24:14**

*They are given the seal of the *"living God."*

*Twelve thousand from each of the twelve tribes of Israel are sealed.

"Seal often refers to a signet ring used to press its image into wax melted on a document. The resulting imprint implied authenticity and ownership and protected the contents."
John Macarthur[57]

*This seal represents the following:

A. **Possession** – Possessed by God

B. **Protection** – Protected by God

C. **Preservation** – Preserved by God

*As Christians we have been sealed as well.

"In whom ye also trusted, after that ye heard the word of truth, the gospel of your salvation: in whom also after that ye believed, ye were sealed with that Holy Spirit of promises."
Ephesians 1:13 KJV

"And grieve not the Holy Spirit of God, whereby ye are sealed unto the day of redemption." **Ephesians 4:30 KJV**

V. THE SERVICE OF THE 144,000 – verse 3

*These 144,000 are called *"servants."*

*It is a privilege to be a servant of God.

*We are all called to be servants of Almighty God.

*Serve the Lord . . .

A. <u>Personally</u>
   *The Apostle Paul
   "Paul, a servant of Jesus Christ, called to be an apostle,
   separated unto the gospel of God." **Romans 1:1 KJV**
B. <u>Passionately</u>
   "Not with eyeservice, as menpleasers; but as the servants of
   Christ, doing the will of God from the heart."
   Ephesians 6:6 KJV
C. <u>Faithfully</u>
   "Moreover it is required in stewards, that a man be found
   faithful." **1 Corinthians 4:2 KJV**
D. <u>Gladly</u>
   "Serve the Lord with gladness: come before his presence
   with singing." **Psalm 100:2 KJV**

*The 144,000 remind us that we are to be witnesses and
 missionaries for Christ as we strive to fulfill the Great
 Commission (Matthew 28:19, 20).
*We must always remember that we have a responsibility to
 share the gospel message wherever we go.
"But if our gospel be hid, it is hid to them that are lost."
2 Corinthians 4:3 KJV

"We've a story to tell to the nations,
That shall turn their hearts to the right,
A story of truth and mercy,
A story of peace and light,
A story of peace and light.
For the darkness shall turn to dawning,
And the dawning to noonday bright,
And Christ's great kingdom shall come to earth,
The kingdom of love and light."
H. Ernest Nichol[58]

"HOMECOMING IN HEAVEN"
Revelation 7:9-17
*This passage gives us glimpse into Heaven.

*Most sermons that deal with the PLACE called Heaven. This message will deal with the INHABITANTS of Heaven.
*This passage is primarily a reference to the saints who come out of the Great Tribulation Period.
*It also applies to all the redeemed of God – verse 14.
*It is important to understand that this world is not our home.
"Dear beloved, I beseech you as strangers and pilgrims, abstain from fleshly lusts, which war against the soul." **1 Peter 2:11 KJV**
"In my Father's house are many mansions: if it were not so, I would have told you. I go to prepare a place for you." **John 14:2 KJV**

"This world is not my home
I'm just a passing through
My treasures are laid up somewhere beyond the blue
The angels beckon me from heaven's open door
And I can't feel at home in this world anymore"[59]

I. THE PEOPLE IN HEAVEN
*These are the citizens of Heaven.
"For our citizenship is in heaven: from whence also we look for the Savior, the Lord Jesus Christ." **Philippians 3:20 KJV**
A. **Their Diversity**
B. **Their Unity** – **verses 9, 14**
C. **Their Purity** – **verse 14**
D. **Their Harmony**
"And they sung a new song, saying, Thou art worthy to take the book: for thou wast slain, and hast redeemed us to God by thy blood out of every kindred, and tongue, and people and nation." **Revelation 5:9 KJV**
*Key word – FAMILY!

"You will notice we say
'brother and sister' round here –
It's because we're a family
And these folks are so near;
When one has a heartache
We all share the tears,
And rejoice in each victory
In this family so dear.

I'm so glad I'm a part of the family of God –
I've been washed in the fountain,
Cleansed by His blood!
Joint heirs with Jesus as we travel this sod;
For I'm part of the family, the family of God."
Bill and Gloria Gaither[60]

II. THE PRAISE IN HEAVEN - Verses 10-12

*There praise is focused on the Lamb – The Lamb is mentioned at least four times.

"You alone are the LORD. You made the heavens, even the highest heavens, and all their starry host, the earth and all that is on it, the seas and all that is in them. You give life to everything, and the multitudes of heaven worship you."
Nehemiah 9:6 NIV

*They worship the . . .
A. <u>Position of God</u> – verse 10
B. <u>Person of God</u> – verse 11 – *"God"*
C. <u>Power of God</u> – verse 12
D. <u>Permanence of God</u> – verse 12

III. THE PLEASURE IN HEAVEN - Verses 16 and 17

"Thou wilt show me the path of life: in thy presence is fullness of joy; at they right hand there are pleasures forevermore." **Psalm 16:11 KJV**

A. <u>Contentment</u>

"As for me, I will behold thy face in righteousness: I shall be satisfied, when I awake, with thy likeness."
Psalm 17:15 KJV

*Every need will be met in Christ.
"Living fountains of waters"
"And the Spirit and the bride say, Come. And let him that heareth say, Come. And let him that is athirst come. And whosoever will, let him take the water of life freely."
Revelation 22:17 KJV

B. Comfort

"And God shall wipe away all tears from their eyes; and there shall be no more death, neither sorrow, nor crying, neither shall there be any more pain: for the former things are passed away." **Revelation 21:4 KJV**

"There's a land that is fairer than day
And by faith we can see it a-far
For the Father waits over the way
To prepare us a dwelling place there

We shall sing on that beautiful shore
The melodious songs of the blessed
And their spirits shall sorrow no more
Not a sigh for the blessings of rest

In the sweet by and by
We shall meet on that beautiful shore
In the sweet by and by
We shall meet on that beautiful shore."[61]

"THE TRUMPET JUDGMENTS OF GOD"
Revelation 8:1-9:21

*When the seventh seal is opened the seven trumpet judgments of God begin.
*Note the following:

I. THE SILENCE IN HEAVEN – verse 1

*Heaven is never silent until now.
*It is an "OH NO" moment.
*God's wrath is about to be unleashed in a terrible way.
*It is the silence before the storm.

A. The Possession of the Trumpets – verse 2

*Seven trumpets are given to seven angels.
*They prepare themselves to sound their trumpets – verse 6.
*Trumpets are often associated with the judgment of God.

55

"Blow ye the trumpet in Zion, and sound an alarm in my
holy mountain: let all the inhabitants of the land tremble:
for the day of the Lord cometh, for it is nigh at hand; A day
of darkness and of gloominess, a day of clouds and of thick
darkness . . . ." **Joel 2:1, 2**

B. **The Prayers of the Saints** – verses 3-5

*An angel has a golden censor of incense which is symbolic
of the prayers of the saints of God.

*These prayers are presented before the throne of God.

*God is about to answer the prayers of the saints in
Revelation 6:9-11.

II. **THE SOUNDING OF THE TRUMPETS**

*The first four trumpets are directed to nature, and the last three
are directed to mankind.

A. **First Trumpet** – verse 7

*Hail and fire mingled with blood.

*Hail mingled with fire was one of the judgments that God
brought against Egypt – Exodus 9:18-25.

*One-third of the trees were destroyed, and all the grass was
burnt up.

*This judgment is directed towards earth's vegetation.

B. **Second Trumpet** – verses 8, 9

"Great mountain" was cast into the sea.

"A great mountain burning with fire likely describes a
colossal meteor hurled into the sea by God."
Daniel Green in the *Moody Bible Commentary*[62]

*One-third of the sea became blood, one-third of the sea
animals died, and one-third of the ships are destroyed.

C. **Third Trumpet** – verses 10, 11

*A star named, *"Wormwood,"* falls from heaven that
devastates the fresh water.

*One-third of the fresh water is contaminated and becomes
wormwood.

D. **Fourth Trumpet** – verse 12

*One-third of the sun, moon, and stars are darkened.

*This trumpet judgment is directed to the heavenly bodies.

A WOE OF WARNING – VERSE 13
One *"woe"* for each of the remaining trumpets.
The Worst is Yet to Come!

E. <u>Fifth Trumpet</u> – verses 9:1-12

*We must view chapter nine (Trumpets Five and Six) as demon activity and attacks.

*This chapter reminds us of the dark and demonic realm of Satan.

"For we wrestle not against flesh and blood, but against principalities, against powers, against the rulers of the darkness of this world, against spiritual wickedness in high places." **Ephesians 6:12 KJV**

*These demonic forces are . . .

1. Hideous
2. Horrible
3. Hellish

*These verses are very difficult to interpret.

"It is probable that, apart from the exact identification of Babylon in chapters 17 and 18, the meaning of the two judgments in this chapter represent the most difficult major problem in the Revelation."

Dr. Wilbur Smith[63]

*The *"star"* refers to a fallen angel cast out of heaven to earth. Possibly a reference to Satan. He is given a key to open the bottomless pit.

*Demonic forces are unleashed upon the earth when it is opened.

1. *Their Assignment* – verses 4, 5

*Their assignment is to torment the unsealed (lost) inhabitants of the earth for five months – verse 10

*They have a commander – verse 11.

2. *Their Appearance*

a. Locust like creatures – verse 3

*The eighth plague in Egypt was locust (Exodus 10:1-20).

*Locusts were often used to bring judgment by God
– Deuteronomy 28:38, 42.
b. Like horses prepared for battle – verse 7
c. Crowns of gold – verse 7
d. Faces of men – verse 7
e. Hair like a woman – verse 8
f. Teeth like a lion – verse 8
g. Breast plates like iron – verse 9
h. Wings that have the sound of chariots – verse 9

3. *Their Affliction*
*These creatures will afflict mankind with the sting of a
scorpion for five month – verses 3, 5, 10.
*Five months (May to September) is the normal life
span of a locust.[64]

F. <u>Sixth Trumpet</u> – verses 13-19
*Four bound demons are released from the Euphrates River
– verse 14.
*The Euphrates River is one of the four rivers that flowed
through the Garden of Eden (Genesis 2:14).
*These demonic creatures are released as a part of God's
divine plan – verse 15.

1. *Their Description*
a. Breastplate of fire – verse 17
b. Heads of lions – verse 17
c. Fire, smoke, and brimstone (weapons of hell) out of
their mouths – verse 17
d. Tails like serpents

2. *Their Destruction* – verses 15, 16
*They destroy one-third of mankind with their army of
two hundred million.

III. THE STUBBORNNESS OF MANKIND – verses 20, 21
A. <u>Their Refusal</u> – verse 20
*Mankind refuses to repent.
"He, that being often reproved hardeneth his neck, shall
suddenly be destroyed, and that without remedy."
Proverbs 29:1 KJV

B. Their Rebellion – verse 21

*Their sins of idolatry, murder, sorcery (drug usage), sexual immorality, stealing, etc. keep them from repenting.

*Don't be stubborn. Let Jesus come into your heart.

"If you are tired of the load of your sin,
Let Jesus come into your heart:
If you desire a new life to begin,
Let Jesus come into your heart."
Leila Naylor Morris[65]

"THE MIGHTY ANGEL"
Revelation 10:1-11

*This is another interlude within the Book of Revelation.

*It is a break in the action before the seventh trumpet sounds leading into the vial/bowl judgments.

*The judgments of God are in series.

*Note the following:

I. THE APPEARANCE OF THE ANGEL–verses 1-4

*He is described as a *"Mighty Angel"* – verse 1

A. Clothed with a Cloud – verse 1

"Cloud" refers to holiness, purity, and the presence of God.

*Tabernacle in the Wilderness

"Then a cloud covered the tent of the congregation, and the glory of the Lord filled the tabernacle. And Moses was not able to enter into the tent of the congregation, because the cloud abode thereon, and the glory of the Lord filled the tabernacle." **Exodus 40:34, 35 KJV**

B. Rainbow Upon His Head – verse 1

"Rainbow" refers to the mercy of God.

*God is merciful.

"The Lord is merciful and gracious, slow to anger, and plenteous in mercy." **Psalm 103:8 KJV**

*God's covenant to Noah was sealed with a rainbow.

"I do set my bow in the cloud, and it shall be a token of a covenant between me and the earth." **Genesis 9:13 KJV**

59

C. <u>**Face was as the Sun**</u> – **verse 1**

"Sun" refers to glory and the splendor of a person.

*Jesus had the face of the sun at the transfiguration.

"And was transfigured before them: and his face did shine as the sun, and his raiment was white as the light."
Matthew 17:2 KJV

*Jesus in Revelation

". . . and his countenance was as the sun shineth in his strength." **Revelation 1:16 KJV**

D. <u>**Feet as Pillars of Fire**</u> – **verse 1**

"Fire" refers to judgment, wrath, and justice.

"For our God is a consuming fire." **Hebrews 12:29 KJV**

*Jesus in Revelation

"And his feet like unto fine brass, as if they burned in a furnace; and his voice as the sound of many waters."
Revelation 1:15 KJV

E. <u>**Possessed a Little Book**</u> – **verse 2**

*In Revelation 5 there is a sealed book that no one could open. It is open at last!

*This book/scroll is the title deed of earth and God's final judgments are revealed.

*God's plan for the ages is contained in the book/scroll.

"And he said, Go thy way, Daniel: for the words are closed up and sealed till the time of the end." **Daniel 12:9 KJV**

F. <u>**His Position**</u> – **verse 2**

"Right foot upon the sea and left foot on the earth"

*This posture symbolizes possession.

*He is ready to take the earth out of the hands of Satan.

*It ultimately refers to the authority and power of Christ.

*God is about to take back what Adam lost in the fall.

G. <u>**Roared Like a Lion**</u> – **verses 3, 4**

*Cry of victory and power.

*A lion is an animal of power.

". . . Behold, the Lion of the tribe of Juda, the Root of David, hath prevailed to open the book, and to loose the seven seals thereof." **Revelation 5:5 KJV**

*This angel is standing with the courage, vengeance, and the judgment of God.

"Seven thunders" – verses 3, 4

*These seven thunders are full of secrecy. John is not allowed to write their meaning. One of the mysteries of Revelation.

II. THE ANNOUNCEMENT OF THE ANGEL – verses 5-7
*The angel makes an oath to God by raising his right hand.
*The angel acknowledges the awesomeness of God – verse 6.
"Thou, even thou, art Lord alone: thou hast made heaven, the heaven of heavens, with all their hosts, the earth, and all things that are therein, the seas, and all that is therein, and thou preservest them all; and the host of heaven worshippeth thee."
Nehemiah 9:6 KJV
*The oath and declaration are that *"there will be no more delay in time"* – verse 6
"The word that is translated *time* actually means 'delay.' God has been delaying His judgments so that lost sinners will have time to repent (2 Peter 3:1-9); now, however, He will accelerate His judgments and accomplish His purposes."
Warren W. Wiersbe[66]
*Now, there will be no more waiting and lingering. God's judgment will be unleashed upon the earth.
*The *"mystery of God"* is about to be revealed.
"Mystery" – sacred secret, the truth and plan of God are about to be fully revealed.
*The full revelation of Christ is about to be known.

III. THE ASSIGNMENT OF THE ANGEL – verses 8-11
*The angel gives to John an assignment.
A. John is to Digest the Book – verse 8-10
*John's assignment was to get the message of the *"little book"* inside of him.
*The book was sweet in his mouth and bitter in his belly.
*The message of the book contained salvation (sweetness) and wrath (bitterness).
B. John is to Declare the Book – verse 11
*John was to preach and proclaim its contents to the entire world.

61

*John's actions towards the *"Little Book"* reminds us as Christians how we should respond to the Bible.

1. We are to Digest the Bible

"Let the word of Christ dwell in you richly . . . ."

Colossians 3:16 KJV

*We digest God's Word by studying it (2 Timothy 2:15), meditating on it (Psalm 1:2), memorizing it (Psalm 119:11), and apply it (James 1:22).

2. We are to Declare the Bible

*We are to share God's Word with others.

"Therefore they that were scattered abroad went every where preaching the word." **Acts 8:4 KJV**

*"Holy Bible, Book Divine,
Precious treasure thou art mine."*
John Burton, Sr.[67]

"THE FUTURE TEMPLE"
Revelation 11:1, 2

*These verses reveal several important truths.

*There have been two Temples in Jerusalem.

1. Solomon's Temple – 1 Kings 8

*It was destroyed by Nebuchadnezzar in 586 B. C.

2. Zerubbabel's Temple – Ezra 3

*It was reconstructed on the original Temple's site. King Herod later expanded and beautified Zerubbabel's Temple. This was the Temple during the time of Jesus. It was destroyed by the Roman General Titus in 70 A. D.

*There will be a future Temple built during the Tribulational Period and the sacrificial system will be reinstituted.

I. THE CERTAINTY OF THE TEMPLE – verse 1

*John is instructed to measure the Temple in Jerusalem with a reed.

*The fact that John was instructed to measure this Temple shows its reality.

"A reed was a hollow, bamboo-like cane plant that grew in the Jordan Valley. Because of its light weight and rigidity, it was commonly used as a measuring rod." **John MacArthur**[68]

II. THE CONGREGATION OF THE TEMPLE – verse 1, 2
*The Temple is specifically dedicated to the Jews (verse 1) and not the Gentiles (verse 2).
*God is not finished with His chosen people the Jews.
*The Tribulation is a period of time that God primarily deals with the Jews.
*The Gentiles will persecute the Jews and Jerusalem for three and one-half years (last half of the Tribulation).

III. THE CORRUPTION OF THE TEMPLE – verse 2
*The Antichrist will use the Temple for his own evil purposes.
*Antichrist will corrupt and pollute the Temple.
"Let no man deceive you by any means; for that day shall not come, except there come a falling away first, and that man of sin be revealed, the son of perdition. Who opposeth and exalteth himself above all that is called God, or that is worshipped; so that he as God sitteth in the temple of God, shewing himself that he is God."
2 Thessalonians 2:3, 4 KJV
*This is known as the *"Abomination of Desolation."*
"And from the time that the daily sacrifice shall be taken away, and the abomination that maketh desolate set up, there shall be a thousand three hundred and five and thirty days."
Daniel 12:11 KJV
"Then he shall confirm a covenant with many for one week; But in the middle of the week He shall bring an end to sacrifice and offering. And on the wing of abominations shall be one who makes desolate, even until the consummation, which is determined, is poured out on the desolate."
Daniel 9:27 NKJV
*Jesus also referred to this *"abomination"* and pollution in Matthew 24:15.

*The future Temple reminds us that we are the Temple of God.
*God resides in the heart of every Believer.

"What? Know ye not that your body is the temple of the Holy Ghost which is in you, which ye have of God, and ye are not your own? For ye are bought with a price: therefore glorify God in your body, and in your spirit, which are God's." **1 Corinthians 6:19, 20 KJV**

"Take my life, and let it be
Consecrated, Lord, to Thee.
Take my moments and my days;
Let them flow in ceaseless praise."
Frances R. Havergal[69]

"THE TWO WITNESSES"
Revelation 11:3-19

*Who are these two witnesses?

*These two witnesses are Elijah and Moses.

1. Elijah – verse 6

*Elijah prayed it would not rain and it didn't rain for three and one-half years – James 5:17-18

"Behold, I will send you Elijah the prophet before the of coming of the great and dreadful day of the Lord." **Malachi 4:5 KJV**

2. Moses – verse 6

*The first plague in Egypt was turning the fresh water into blood – Exodus 7:14-21

*Both Moses and Elijah appeared at the transfiguration of Christ – Matthew 17:1-8

I. THE MINISTRY OF THE TWO WITNESSES –
verses 3, 6, 10 – *"Prophets"*

*These two prophets will have a special anointing (verse 4) and authority (verse 6).

*They will prophesy and preach with . . .

A. <u>Conviction</u> – verse 3

"Clothed with sackcloth" – garment worn for confession, repentance, and expressing sorrow.

B. <u>Clarity</u> – verse 4

*Verse 4 refers to them as *"the two olive trees and the two candlesticks"*

*This is a reference to light. Olive oil from the olive trees is

burned in the lampstands. They will be a light or God in a dark world.
C. **Courage**
D. **Confrontation**

II. **THE MURDER OF THE TWO WITNESSES** – verses 7-10
  A. **Their Death** – verse 7
    *They will be killed by the Antichrist.
    *Satan hates God's servants.
  B. **Their Dishonor** – verses 8-10
    *Bodies left in the street – verse 8, 9
    *People will celebrate their death.

III. **THE MIRACLE OF THE TWO WITNESSES** – verses 11, 12
  *These two witnesses are brought back to life.
  A. **Their Resurrection** – verse 11
    *This is a demonstration of the power of God.
  B. **Their Rescue** – verse 12
    *They are rescued by ascending into heaven.
  C. **Their Results** – verse 13
    *Their lives and ministry made a tremendous impact.
    *The remanent gave glory to God.

*As Christians lets be a light and a witness to this dark world that desperately needs the gospel.
"Let your light so shine before men, that they may see your good works, and glorify your Father which is in heaven."
Matthew 5:16 KJV

"Shine, Jesus, shine
Fill this land with the Father's glory
Blaze, Spirit, blaze
Set our hearts on fire
Flow, river, flow
Flood the nations with grace and mercy
Send forth your word
Lord, and let there be light."
Graham Kendrick[70]

"THE TRUMPET OF TRIUMPH"
Revelation 11:14-19

*In these verses the last trumpet sounds and immediately the focus is placed upon Almighty God and the Lord Jesus Christ.
*Note the following:

I. THE ACKNOWLEDMENT – verse 15
*The voices of heaven acknowledge the following:

A. The Sovereignty of Christ

B. The Supremacy of Christ

*Christ is sovereign and supreme in the universe.

*He reigns for eternally.

"God reigneth over the heathen: God sitteth upon the throne of his holiness." **Psalm 47:8 KJV**

"Before the mountains were brought forth, or ever thou hadst formed the earth and the world, even from everlasting to everlasting, thou art God." **Psalm 90:2 KJV**

II. THE ADORATION – verse 16, 17
*The twenty-four elders worship Almighty God.

*Their worship involves three things:

A. Reverence – verse 16

"Fell upon their faces"

*Reverence is essential to worship.

"Let all the earth fear the Lord: let all the inhabitants of the world stand in awe of him." **Psalm 33:8 KJV**

"O come, let us worship and bow down: let us kneel before the Lord our maker." **Psalm 95:6 KJV**

B. Worship – verse 16

"O worship the Lord in the beauty of holiness: fear before him, all the earth." **Psalm 96:9 KJV**

"God is a Spirit: and they that worship him must worship him in spirit and truth." **John 4:24 KJV**

C. Thanksgiving – verse 17

"It is a good thing to give thanks unto the Lord, and to sing praises unto thy name, O most High." **Psalm 92:1 KJV**

"Enter into his gates with thanksgiving, and into his courts with praise: be thankful unto him, and bless his name."
Psalm 100:4 KJV

III. THE ANGER – verse 18
A. The Nations are Angry
*The Nations are angry out of Selfishness.
*Read Psalm 2
B. God is Angry
*God is angry out of righteousness.
"God judgeth the righteous, and God is angry with the wicked every day." **Psalm 7:11 KJV**

IV. THE ARK – verse 18
*The ark of the covenant is mentioned.
*The ark is significant because it represents the following:
A. The Presence of God
*The Ark was a visible representation of God's presence (Leviticus 16:2).
B. The Purity of God
*The Ark of the Covenant was kept in the "Holy of Holies." (Hebrews 9:3, 4)
C. The Pardon of God
*Once a year on the Day of Atonement (Yom Kippur) the High Priest would sprinkle blood over the Mercy Seat (lid of the Ark of the Covenant) to atone for the sins of the people. The Day of Atonement was on the tenth day of the seventh month.
*God is a forgiving God.
"For thou, Lord, art good and ready to forgive and plenteous in mercy unto all them that call upon thee."
Psalm 86:5 KJV
*Jesus Christ gave the ultimate sacrifice for our sins and forgiveness.
"Neither by the blood of goats and calves, but by his own blood he entered in once into the holy place, having obtained eternal redemption for us."
Hebrews 9:12 KJV

"Come, thou almighty King,
Help us thy name to sing,
Help us to praise!
Father all glorious,
O'er all victorious,
Come and reign over us,
Ancient of Days!"
Anonymous[71]

"ISRAEL - GOD'S CHOSEN PEOPLE"
Revelation 12:1-17

*One of the emphases of this chapter is Israel.

*Israel is God's chosen people. God is not finished with the Jews!

*The Tribulation Period is God's last dealings with His chosen
people.

*The Tribulation Period is the 70th week of Daniel which is
mentioned in Daniel 9:27. (See also Daniel 9:24.)

"Alas! For that day is great, so that none is like it: it is even time of
Jacob's trouble; but he shall be saved out of it."

Jeremiah 30:7 KJV

I. THE PRECIOUSNESS OF ISRAEL

*The Jews are precious to Almighty God.

". . . for he that toucheth you toucheth the apple of his eye."

Zechariah 2:8 KJV

"And I will bless them that bless thee, and curse him that curseth
thee: and in thee shall all families of the earth be blessed."

Genesis 12:3 KJV

"For thou art an holy people unto the Lord thy God: the Lord
thy God hath chosen thee to be a special people unto himself,
above all people that are upon the face of the earth. The Lord
did not set his love upon you, nor choose you, because ye were
more in number than any people: for ye were the fewest of
all people; But because the Lord loved you, and because he
would keep the oath which he had sworn unto your fathers,
hath the Lord brought you out with a mighty hand, and
redeemed you out of the house of bondman, from the hand of
Pharaoh king of Egypt." **Deuteronomy 7:6-8 KJV**

*The Jews are a . . .
A. <u>Sacred People</u>
B. <u>Special People</u>
C. <u>Separated People</u>

II. THE PORTRAYAL OF ISRAEL – verses 1, 2
*Israel is often portrayed as a woman in Scripture.
"For your Maker is your husband, the Lord of hosts is His
name; and your Redeemer is the Holy One of Israel; He is
called the God of the whole earth. For the Lord has called you
like a woman forsaken and grieved in spirit, like a youthful
wife when you were refused, says your God."
Isaiah 54:5, 6 NKJV
*In this passage she is described as a pregnant woman.
*She is clothed with the sun, the moon under her feet, and
wearing a crown of twelve stars – verse 1.
*This parallels the dream of Joseph in Genesis 37:9-11.
*The twelve stars represent the twelve tribes of Israel.[72]

III. THE PROMISE TO ISRAEL – verse 5
*God promises the Jewish people that the Messiah would
come.
*This child is Jesus Christ.
"For unto us a child is born, unto us a son is given: and the
government shall be upon his shoulder: and his name shall be
called Wonderful, Counselor, The Mighty God, The
everlasting Father, The Prince of Peace. Of the increase of
his government and peace there shall be no end, upon the
throne of David, and upon his kingdom, to order it, and to
establish it with judgment and with justice from henceforth
even for ever. The zeal of the Lord of hosts will perform
this." **Isaiah 9:6, 7 KJV**

IV. THE PERSECUTION OF ISRAEL – verses 6, 13
*The red dragon persecutes the woman.
*The dragon is Satan. (See next lesson.)
*God's people have always been a persecuted people.

"Sing, O heavens; and be joyful, O earth; and break forth into
singing, O mountains: for the Lord hath comforted his
people, and will have mercy upon his afflicted."
Isaiah 49:13 KJV

V. THE PRESERVATION OF ISRAEL – verses 14-17
Eagles Wings" – **verses 14** is also used in God's deliverance
of the Hebrews from Pharaoh.
"Ye have seen what I did unto the Egyptians, how I bare you on
eagles' wings, and brought you unto myself."
Exodus 19:4 KJV
*The *"flood"* in **verses 15, 16** refers to Satan's flood of hatred
and antisemitism towards the Jewish people.
*Key word is *"remnant"* – **verse 17**
*God always has a remnant of His people.
"And I will gather the remnant of my flock out of all countries
whither I have driven them, and will bring them again to their
folds; and they shall be fruitful and increase."
Jeremiah 23:3 KJV

*God's people are special.
*As Christians we are very special to the Lord just like the Jews.
"But you are a chosen generation, a royal priesthood a holy nation,
His own special people, that you may proclaim the praises of Him
who called you out of darkness into His marvelous light."
1 Peter 2:9 NKJV

"God the Father of Your people,
You have called us to be one;
Grant us grace to walk together
In the joy of Christ, Your Son.
Challenged by Your Word and Spirit,
Blest with gifts from heav'n above;
As one body we will serve You,
And bear witness to Your love."
Alfred E. Mulder[73]

"THE FALL OF SATAN"
Revelation 12:1-17

*Satan is the source of all sin and wickedness.

*Revelation 12:1-7 helps us understand where Satan came from.

*As Christians we are reminded that Satan is our enemy and adversary.

"Be sober, be vigilant; because your adversary the devil, as a roaring lion, walketh about, seeking whom he may devour."
1 Peter 5:8 KJV

I. THE REALITY OF SATAN – verse 3

*This *"great red dragon"* refers to Satan – **verse 9**

*Satan is a real being.

*He is wicked.

*Satan is behind all of the evil in the world and will certainly be unleased during the Tribulation Period.

*Satan is known by numerous titles in the Bible. Each of these titles describe his Character and nature.

1. Lucifer – Isaiah 14:12
2. Adversary – 1 Peter 5:8
3. Devil – Revelation 12:9, James 4:7
4. Wicked One – Matthew 13:19
5. Murderer – John 8:44
6. Liar – John 8:44
7. God of the world – 2 Corinthians 4:4
8. Prince of this world – John 12:31, John 14:30
9. Ruler of Darkness – Ephesians 6:12
10. The Dragon – Revelation 12:9
11. Accuser of the Brethren – Revelation 12:10, Revelation 20:2
12. Serpent – Genesis 3:1, Revelation 12:9, Revelation 20:2

II. THE REBELLION OF SATAN – verses 7, 8

*Satan in his original state was known as Lucifer (Isaiah 14:12).

A. The Devil is a Created Being

71

"Thou art the anointed cherub that covereth; and I have set thee so: thou wast upon the holy mountain of God; thou hast walked up and down in the midst of the stones of fire. Thou wast perfect in thy ways from the day that thou wast created, till iniquity was found in thee."
Ezekiel 28:14, 15 KJV

B. The Devil is a Corrupted Being

*The Devil was corrupted by the sin of pride.

"How art thou fallen from heaven, O Lucifer, son of the morning! How art thou cut down to the ground, which didst weaken the nations! For thou hast said in thine heart, I will ascend into heaven, I will exalt my throne above the stars of God: I will sit also upon the mount of the congregation, in the sides of the north: I will ascend above the heights of the clouds; I will be like the most High."
Isaiah 14:12-14 KJV

III. THE REMOVAL OF SATAN – verse 9

*Satan's removal from Heaven is mentioned in Isaiah 14:15.

"Yet thou shalt be brought down to hell, to the sides of the pit."
Isaiah 14:15 KJV

*When Satan was ejected and removed from Heaven he took one-third of the angels with him – verse 4.

*These fallen angels are now demonic forces (Ephesians 6:12).

IV. THE RAMPAGE OF SATAN – verse 12

*Satan knows he has but a short time.

"The thief cometh not, but for to steal, and to kill, and to destroy . . . ." **John 10:10 KJV**

*He will especially work havoc and chaos during the Tribulation Period.

V. THE RESISTANCE OF SATAN – verse 11

*We must never forget that we are soldiers of the Lord. We are in God's army.

"You therefore must endure hardness as a good soldier of Jesus Christ. No one engaged in warfare entangles himself with the affairs of this life, that he may please him who enlisted him as a soldier." **2 Timothy 2:3, 4 NKJV**

*This verse mentions
   1. Blood of the Lamb
   2. Word of their Testimony
   3. Surrendered Life to Christ
"Submit yourselves therefore to God. Resist the devil, and he will flee from you." **James 4:7 KJV**
*TEMPTATION OF JESUS in the wilderness –
   Matthew 4:1-11. Jesus RESISTED Satan.
*In Christ we are VICTORS and not VICTIMS.
"But thanks be to God, which giveth us the victory through our Lord Jesus Christ." **1 Corinthains 15:57 KJV**
"Nay, in all these things we are more than conquerors through him that loved us." **Romans 8:37 KJV**
"WE ARE NOT FIGHTING FOR VICTORY WE ARE FIGHTING FROM VICTORY!"
"He that committeth sin is of the devil; for this purpose the Son of God was manifested, that he might destroy the works of the devil." **1 John 3:8 KJV**
"Forasmuch then as the children are partakers of flesh and blood, he also himself likewise took part of the same, that through death he might destroy him that had power of death, that is the devil." **Hebrews 2:14 KJV**
*Our victory comes from the PERSON, POWER, and PROVISION of Jesus Christ.
*In order to resist Satan we must be . . .
A. **Watchful** – 1 Peter 5:8
B. **Prayerful** – Ephesians 6:18,
   1 Thessalonians 5:17
C. **Forceful** – James 4:7
   *We must wear the Armor of God – Ephesians 6:12-18

*"At the sign of triumph
Satan's host doth flee;
On then Christian soldiers,
On to victory!
Hell's foundations quiver
At the shout of praise;
Brothers, life your voices,
Loud your anthems raise.*

Onward, Christian soldiers,
Marching as to war,
With the cross of Jesus
Going on before."
Sabine Baring-Gould[74]

"THE RISE OF THE ANTICHRIST"
Revelation 13:1, 2

*The word, *"Antichrist,"* (*antichristos* in the Greek) can mean either against Christ or instead of Christ, or a combination of the two.[75]

*The Antichrist will oppose Christ and he will be a substitute, counterfeit Christ.

*Throughout history there have been those who have tried to identify the Antichrist.

*Some have suggested the following historical figures: Caesar, Nero, Napoleon, Hitler, Mussolini, Vladimir Putin, etc.

*Attempts to identify the Antichrist are useless and futile.

*We must not be sensational, but Scriptural.

*What does the Bible reveal about this individual known as the Antichrist?

I. THE PERSONALITY OF THE ANTICHRIST

*The Antichrist is a person. He is not a world system or philosophy.

*Dr. David Jeremiah describes the Antichrist as a charismatic, cunning, and cruel leader.[76]

A. His Description

*Throughout the Bible we find a number of references and titles that describe his character and nature. He is evil.

*Verse 1 – *"out of the sea"*

"The sea represents the abyss or pit, the haunt of demons (11:7, 17:8, 20:1, and Luke 8:31)."
John MacArthur[77]

1. *"Man of Sin"* – 2 Thessalonians 2:3
2. *"Son of Perdition"* – 2 Thessalonians 2:3
3. *"Wicked One"* – 2 Thessalonians 2:8

4. *"Vile Person"* – Daniel 11:21
   *Some have suggested that the Antichrist may be a homosexual based on Daniel 11:37
   "Neither shall he regard the God of his fathers, nor desire of women, nor regard any god: for he shall magnify himself above all." **Daniel 11:37 KJV**
5. *"Beast"* – Revelation 13:1
   *He is described in verse 2
   "Like unto a leopard" – Swiftness
   *Rise to power will be swift.
   "Feet of a bear" – Strength
   *Crush his opponents.
   "Mouth of a lion" – Power
   *Devour anyone who stands in his way.

B. <u>His Deception</u> – verse 3, 12
   *He will deceive the world through a counterfeit resurrection.
   *He will be a great orator.
   *The Bible reveals how he will deceive the world through communication.
   *Adolf Hitler was able to deceive many through his oratory and communication skills.
   *The Antichrist will use the following:
   1. *"Lies"* – 2 Thessalonians 2:9-11
   2. *"Speak Great Things"* – Revelation 13:5
   3. *"Blasphemies"* – Revelation 13:6
   4. *"Flatteries"* – Daniel 11:21
   *He will establish a covenant with the Jews which he will break halfway through the Tribulation Period (Daniel 9:24-27).
   *The Temple will be rebuilt according to 2 Thessalonians 2:4.

II. THE POWER OF THE ANTICHRIST
   *The Antichrist gets his power from Satan (the dragon) – verse 4.
   "And his power shall be mighty, but not his own power: and he shall destroy wonderfully, and shall prosper, and practice, and shall destroy the mighty and holy people." **Daniel 8:24 KJV**

*Verse 1 refers to kingdoms and nations.
  (See Daniel 7:24 and Revelation 17:12)
*He will be a powerful individual and leader.
*He will be charismatic and popular.
1. He will be a brilliant genius and philosopher – Daniel 8:23
2. He will be a great military leader – Revelation 6:1, 2 and
   Revelation 13:4
3. He will be a crafty politician – Daniel 8:25
*Note the following about the power of the Antichrist.
A. The Scope of His Power – "Worldwide"
  *He will be able to rule the entire world.
  "And power was given him over all kindreds, and tongues,
  and nations." **Revelation 13:7, b KJV**
B. The Source of His Power – verse 2
  *He receives his power from Satan.
  "Even him, whose coming is after the working of Satan with
  all power and signs and lying wonders."
  2 Thessalonians 2:9 KJV

III. THE PLAN OF THE ANTICHRIST
*The Antichrist has a threefold plan or agenda.
**A. To Engage in Persecution of the Jews and the
  Tribulational Saints** – verse 7, 10
  *He will establish a covenant with the Jews which he will
  break midway through the Tribulation Period (Daniel
  9:24-27).
  *The Antichrist will hate anything associated with God thus
  he will persecute Jews and the Tribulational saints.
B. To Enforce a World-Wide Identification Mark
  (Revelation 13:16-18)
  *All will be required to have an identification mark. The
  mark indicates that the one bearing it both worships the
  beast and submits to his rule. It indicates allegiance and
  loyalty.
  *The mark is mentioned seven times in the book of
  Revelation:
  1. Revelation 13:16-18
  2. Revelation 14:9
  3. Revelation 14:11

4. Revelation 15:2
5. Revelation 16:2
6. Revelation 19:20
7. Revelation 20:4
   *The Antichrist will set up a world-wide economic system based on the number 666.
   *Seven is the number of perfection, but six is one short of perfection – trinity of imperfection (Satan, Antichrist, and the False Prophet).
C. <u>To Exalt Himself as God</u> – verses 4, 8
   *During the Tribulation Period people will worship both Satan and the Antichrist.
   *Satan has always desired to be worshipped. This is seen in his rebellion and fall (Isaiah 14:12-14) and the temptation of Christ (Matthew 4:8-10). Satan will receive worship through the person of the Antichrist.
   "Who opposeth and exalteth himself above all that is called God, or that is worshiped; so that he as God sitteth in the temple of God, showing himself that he is God."
   2 Thessalonians 2:4 KJV
   "And the king shall do according to his will; and he shall exalt himself, and magnify himself above every god, and shall speak marvelous things against the God of gods, and shall prosper till the indignation be accomplished: for that is determined shall be done." **Daniel 11:36 KJV**

CONCLUSION
*Antichrist will be a false Christ. He will be a counterfeit.
*Accept the real Christ, JESUS, as your Savior.
"For unto you is born this day in the city of David a Savior, which is Christ the Lord." **Luke 2:11 KJV**
*The Apostle Peter on the Day of Pentecost.
"Therefore let all the house of Israel know assuredly, that God hath made that same Jesus, whom ye have crucified, both Lord and Christ." **Acts 2:36 KJV**

"Don't waste your time looking around for the antichrist, rather spend it looking up for Jesus Christ!" Dr. Gary Frazier[78]

"THE FALSE PROPHET"
Revelation 13:11-15

*The Dragon (Satan), The Antichrist, and the False Prophet will
form an unholy trinity.

*John MacArthur describes the False Prophet as follows:

"Antichrist will be primarily a political and military leader, but the
false prophet will be a religious leader. Politics and religion will
unite in a world-wide religion of worshiping the Antichrist."

John MacArthur[79]

*Note the following about the False Prophet:

I. THE MINISTRY – verse 11

*This second beast is the false prophet – Revelation 16:13,
19:20, and 20:11.

*The False Prophet will be a world religious figure who will
direct worship to the Antichrist.

*He will function as a counterfeit Holy Spirit.

*He will bear witness of the Antichrist.

"Two horns like a lamb" – He will be deceptively gentle and
appealing

"He Spake as a dragon" – Speaks with authority and power

II. THE MONUMENT – verses 14, 15

*The false prophet erects an image or statue of the Beast in the
Temple in Jerusalem.

*This is known as the **"Abomination of Desolation"** – Daniel
9:27, 12:11, Matthew 24:15, and 2 Thessalonians 2:4

III. The MIRACLES – verses 13-15

*The False Prophet will perform great miracles that will
deceive many.

A. Fire from Heaven – verse 13

*Imitates Elijah – 1 Kings 18:38

B. Gives Life to the Image of the Beast – verse 15

IV. THE MANDATE – verses 12, 15

*He will require the inhabitants of the earth to worship the
beast.

*Those who refuse will be killed – verse 15.

V. THE MARK – verses 16-18
  *He will assist in requiring everyone to have an identification mark known as *"The Mark of the Beast."*
  *The mark indicates that the one bearing it both worships the beast and submits to his rule.
  *The Antichrist will set up a world-wide economic system based on the number 666.
  *Seven is the number of perfection, but six is one short of perfection.
  *The Dragon, Antichrist, and False Prophet will form a trinity of imperfection.

*As Christians we are reminded to beware of false prophets.
"Beloved, believe not every spirit, but try the spirits whether they are of God: because many false prophets are gone out into the world."
1 John 4:1
"Be on your guard against false prophets who come to you in sheep's clothing but inwardly are ravaging wolves."
Matthew 7:15 CSB
*The way we resist false prophets and teachers is with the truth of God's Word.
". . . if ye continue in my word, then are ye my disciples indeed; and ye shall know the truth, and the truth shall make you free."
John 8:31, 32 KJV

"My hope is built on nothing less
Than Jesus' blood and righteousness;
I dare not trust the sweetest frame,
But wholly lean on Jesus' name.
On Christ, the solid Rock, I stand;
All other ground is sinking sand,
All other ground is sinking sand."
Edward Mote[80]

"WORSHIP AND WRATH"
Revelation 14:1-20

*This chapter points to events after the Tribulation Period.
*John is looking beyond the Tribulation.
*Note the following in this chapter.

I. THE HOPE – verses 1, 4
*The Lamb is the hope of the world.
*In the midst of the Tribulation the Lamb appears offering hope.
*Jesus is the Lamb of God.
*The Lamb is the hope of the world for the following reasons.

A. <u>His Provision</u>
". . . Behold the Lamb of God, which taketh away the sin of the world." **John 1:29 KJV**

B. <u>His Pardon</u>
"For you know that you were redeemed from your empty way of life inherited from your fathers, not with perishable things like silver and gold, but with the precious blood of Christ, like that of an unblemished and spotless lamb."
1 Peter 3:18, 19 CSB
"In whom we have redemption though his blood, even the forgiveness of sins." **Colossians 1:14 KJV**

C. <u>His Peace</u>
*Only the Lamb can give peace to a human heart and bring peace to this world.
"Therefore being justified by faith, we have peace with God through our Lord Jesus Christ." **Romans 5:1 KJV**
"Prince of Peace" – Isaiah 9:6

II. THE HOST – verses 1-5
*The 144,000 are with the Lamb on Mount Zion.
*We were introduced to them in Revelation 7:1-8.
*Note their . . .

A. <u>Seal</u> – verse 1 – Revelation 7:4
"Father's name in their foreheads"
*We have been sealed by the Holy Spirit.

"In whom ye also trusted, after that ye heard the word of truth, the gospel of your salvation: in whom also, after that ye believed, ye were sealed with that Holy Spirit of promises." **Ephesians 1:13 KJV**

B. <u>Song</u> – verse 3

*As Christians we have been given a song to sing as well – the song of salvation.

"And he hath put a new song in my mouth, even praise unto our God: many shall see it, and fear, and shall trust in the Lord." **Psalm 40:3 KJV**

C. <u>Separation</u> – verses 4, 5

*We are to live a separated for God.

"Wherefore come out from among them, and be ye separate, saith the Lord, and touch not the unclean thing; and I will receive you." **2 Corinthians 6:17 KJV**

III. THE HERALDS – verses 6-18

*At least seven heralding angels appear.

1. Verse 6
2. Verse 8
3. Verse 9
4. Verse 13
5. Verse 15
6. Verse 17
7. Verse 18

*The message of these angels is . . .

A. <u>Clear</u>
B. <u>Critical</u>
C. <u>Challenging</u>
D. <u>Certain</u>

IV. THE HORROR – verses 15-20

*It will be a horrible thing when God's wrath is unleashed upon the earth.

*God's wrath is unleased on the . . .

A. <u>Wicked</u> – verse 9-11
B. <u>World</u> – verses 15-20

*These verses allude to the Battle of Armageddon – Revelation 19:11-21.

*The world desperately needs the **gospel** – **verse 6**
*The *"gospel"* is the good news of Jesus Christ.
"For I am not ashamed of the gospel of Christ: for it is the power of God unto salvation to every one that believeth; to the Jew first, and also to the Greek." **Romans 1:16 KJV**
". . . Go ye into all the world, and preach the gospel to every creature." **Mark 16:15 KJV**

> *"We've a story to tell to the nations.*
> *That shall turn their hearts to the right,*
> *A story of truth and mercy,*
> *A story of peace and light."*
> **H. Ernest Nichol**[81]

"THE VIAL/BOWL JUDGEMENTS OF GOD"
Revelation 15:1-16:21
*Chapters 15 and 16 go together.
*Chapter 15 is a prelude to chapter 16.

I. THE PREPARATION – Revelation 15:1, 5-7
*Seven angels are given seven vials/bowls.
*The content of the vials/bowls is the *"Wrath of God"*
*Verse 6 – These angels are wearing priestly garments.
*These angels are about to do the Holy Work of God.

II. THE PRAISE – Revelation 15:2-4
*The Tribulational saints. See Revelation 12:7
*The Song of Moses is a song of victory.
*The Hebrews sang a song of victory to God after they crossed the Red Sea – Exodus 15:1-19.
*They praise God for His . . .
A. Greatness – verse 3 – *"Great"*
B. Awesomeness – verse 3 – *"Lord God Almighty"*
C. Truthfulness – verse 3 – *"just and true"*
D. Holiness – verse 4 – *"Holy"*
*God is to be continually praised.

"By him therefore let us offer the sacrifice of praise to God continually, that is, the fruit of our lips, giving thanks to his name." **Hebrews 13:5 KJV**

III. THE PRESENCE – verse 8

"Smoke" is symbolic of the presence of God.

1. Moses and Mount Sinai – Exodus 19:18
2. Isaiah in the Temple – Isaiah 6:4

*The smoke reveals the . . .

   A. <u>Mystery of God</u>
   B. <u>Glory of God</u>
   C. <u>Deity of God</u>
   D. <u>Majesty of God</u>

*God's presence is about to be made known to the world through His wrath and judgment.

IV. THE PLAGUES – Revelation 16:1-21

*This chapter contains *"great"* things.

1. *"Great Voice"* – verse 1, 17
2. *"Great Heat"* – verse 9
3. *"Great River Euphrates"* – verse 12
4. *"Great Day of God Almighty"* – verse 14
5. *"Great Earthquake"* – verse 18
6. *"Great City"* – verse 19
7. *"Great Babylon"* – verse 19
8. *"Great Hail"* – verse 21
9. *"Great Plague"* – verse 21

*Verse 1 – Angels are instructed to pour out the wrath of God.

   A. <u>First Vial/Bowl</u> – verse 2
      *Grievous Sores
      *Alludes to the sixth plague in Egypt – Exodus 9:8-12
   B. <u>Second Vial/Bowl</u> – verse 3
      *Sea Turned to Blood
   C. <u>Third Vial/Bowl</u> – verses 4-7
      *Fresh water turned to Blood
      *Alludes to the first plague in Egypt – Exodus 7:14-25
   D. <u>Fourth Vial/Bowl</u> – verses 8, 9
      *Fire and Great Heat from the Sun
   E. <u>Fifth Vial/Bowl</u> – verses 10, 11

*Darkness and Pain
*Alludes to the ninth plague in Egypt – Exodus 10:21-23

F. **Sixth Vial/Bowl** – **verse 12**
*Euphrates River Dries Up
*This is in preparation for the Battle of Armageddon – verses 13-16.

G. **Seventh Vial/Bowl** – **verses 17-21**
*Devasting Earthquake and Large Hail weighing around 100 Pounds.
*Alludes the seventh plague in Egypt – Exodus 9:22-26.

*These plaques are . . .
1. **They are Swift** – **verse 1** – *"poured out"*
2. **They are Severe** – **verse 1** – *"wrath of God"*
3. **They are Scary**

Verse 17 – *"It is Done!"*

---

*"Mine eyes have seen the glory
Of the coming of the Lord;
He is trampling out the vintage
Where the grapes of wrath are stored;
He hath loosed the fateful ligtning
Of His terrible swift sword;
His truth is marching on."*
Julia Ward Howe[82]

"THE FALL OF RELIGIOUS BABYLON"
Revelation 17:1-18

*The next three chapters will involve God's judgment of Satan. "Satan's entire system is now about to be judged by God: his religious system (the harlot – Revelation 17), his political and economic system (Babylon – Revelation 18), and his military system (the armies – Revelation 19)." **Warren W. Wiersbe**[83]
*Revelation is filled with counterfeits.
1. Counterfeit Christ – Antichrist
2. Counterfeit Trinity – Satan, Antichrist, False Prophet
3. Counterfeit Church – Religious Babylon
*The true church will be gone through the rapture.

84

*Note the contrast.
1. **Satan's Church is Polluted**
   *Describe as a *"whore"* (verse 1) and a *"harlot"* (verse 5).
2. **God's Church is a Pure** *– "virgin"*– Revelation 19:7-8,
   2 Corinthians 11:2
*The influence of this corrupt religious system will be world-wide –
verses 1, 15
*Note the following:

I. HER DESCRIPTION
   *Note two things about her.
   ### A. <u>She is Worldly</u>
   *The following words are used to describe her worldliness.
   1. *"Whore"* – verse 1
   2. *"Fornication"* – verse 2
   3. *"Blasphemy"* – verse 3
   4. *"Abominations"* – verse 4
   5. *"Mother of Harlots"* – verse 5
   *Christians and churches must be careful of worldliness.
   "Ye adulterers and adulteresses, know ye not that the
   friendship of the world is enmity with God? Whosoever
   therefore will be a friend of the world is the enemy of
   God." **James 4:4 KJV**
   ### B. <u>She is Wealthy</u> – verses 3, 4
   *Her wealth is revealed by her attire.
   1. *"Arrayed in purple and scarlet"*
   2. *"Decked with gold, precious stones, and pearls"*
   3. *"Golden cup in her hand"*
   *She loves the things of this world.
   "Love not the world, neither the things that are in the world.
   If any man love the world, the love of the Father is not in
   him." **1 John 2:15 KJV**

II. HER DECEPTION – verse 2
   "Made drunk with the wine of her fornication"
   *She intoxicates the world with false doctrine and deception.
   *She blinds with false teachings.
   *We must guard ourselves against false doctrine.

"For there shall arise false Christs, and false prophets, and shall show great signs and wonders; insomuch that, if it were possible, they shall deceive the very elect."
Matthew 24:24 KJV
"For the time will come when they will not endure sound doctrine; but after their own lusts shall they heap to themselves teachers, having itching ears; and they shall turn away their ears from the truth, and shall be turned unto fables."
2 Timothy 4:3, 4 KJV

III. HER DISCIPLES – verses 2, 8-14
*Her disciples will be the *"kings of the earth"* – verse 2.
*This will include the Antichrist and his followers.
*She rides a *"scarlet beast"* – verse 3 which refers to the Antichrist himself.
  1. *"Seven Kings"* – verse 10
        Representative of the seven great world empires (Egypt, Assyria, Babylon, Medo-Persia, Greece, Rome, and the Antichrist). When John wrote, the Egyptian, Assyrian, Babylonian, Medo-Persian, and Greek empires had gone out of existence; Rome still existed; and the Antichrist's empire had not yet come. **John MacArthur[84]**
  2. *"Ten Kings"* – verse 12
        *Antichrist will be a leader of a ten nation federation. The Antichrist will be given authority and power by this alliance.

IV. HER DESIRE – verses 6, 14
*Her goal and desire will be to persecute true Believers (*Saints and Martyrs*).
*Ultimately, she and the world leaders make war with the Lamb – verse 14.

V. HER DOOM – verses 16-18
*The Antichrist and his followers will turn their backs on this religious system and it will cease to exist.
*God will use the Antichrist and the federation of ten nations to extinguish her influence and ministry.

*God's purposes and plans are always achieved.
*It is wonderful to know that the true church of God will never die or cease to exist.

"Like a mighty army
Moves the church of God;
Brothers, we are treading
Where the saints have trod.
We are not divided, all one body we,
On in hope and doctrine,
One in charity."
Sabine Baring-Gould[85]

"THE FALL OF COMMERCIAL BABYLON"
Revelation 18:1-24

"Babylon" – verse 2 – refers to the religious, political, and commercial/economic system of the Antichrist.[86]

I. THE COLLAPSE OF BABYLON – verse 1-8
*The collapse of commercial Babylon will be extremely swift and sudden.
*Described as falling in *"one hour"*– verses 10, 17, 19,
*Babylon is corrupt – verse 2, 3

II. THE CALL OUT OF BABYLON – verse 4
*God calls his people out of the city to separate themselves.
*To reasons for this:
    1. Avoid the Pollution – verse 4
    2. Avoid the Plagues – verse 4
*The call is to *"Come out."*
*As God's people we are called to *"Come Out."*
"Wherefore come out from among them, and be ye separate, saith the Lord, and touch not the unclean thing; and I will receive you." **2 Corinthians 6:17 KJV**

III. THE CRYING FOR BABYLON – verses 9-19
*Notice the words used for crying.

1. *"Bewail"* – verse 9
2. *"Lament"* – verse 9
3. *"Weep"* – verses 11, 15, 19
4. *"Mourn"* – verse 11
5. *"Wailing"* – verse 15, 19

A. **They Cry Over the Loss of Profits**
B. **They Cry Over the Loss of Possessions**
C. **They Cry Over the Loss of Pleasures**

"No one can serve two masters, since either he will hate one and love the other, or he will be devoted to one and despise the other. You cannot serve both God and money." **Matthew 6:24 CSB**

IV. THE CELEBRATION OVER BABYLON – verses 20-24

*All of Heaven celebrates the collapse of Babylon.
*Earth weeps – Heaven rejoices.
*Heaven rejoices over the collapse of Babylon.
*God's Vengeance has been unleashed for the *"blood of the prophets, saints, and the slain."*
". . . Vengeance is mine; I will repay, saith the Lord."
Romans 12:19 KJV

"We shall overcome,
We shall overcome,
We shall overcome someday.

God is on our side,
God is on our side,
God is on our side today.

Oh, deep in our hearts we do believe
We shall overcome someday."
African American Spiritual[87]

"THE MARRIAGE SUPPER OF THE LAMB"
Revelation 19:1-9

*In the western world, the focus of the wedding is on the bride.
*In biblical times the focus was on the groom – verse 7

(Parable of the Ten Virgins – Matthew 25:1-13)

*The focus of the Marriage Supper of the Lamb will be on the person of the Lord Jesus Christ.

*The Marriage Supper of the Lamb reveals the unique relationship that God's people have with the Lord Jesus Christ.

*The Bible reveals the story of Christ's special love for His people – the CHURCH.

*The Church is described as follows in the Bible.

1. **A Building** – 1 Corinthians 3:9, 16 - Symbolic of Strength
2. **A Body** – Colossians 1:18 - Symbolic of Service
3. **A Bride** – Ephesians 5:25-32 - Symbolic of Separation

I. THE PURCHASE OF THE BRIDE – verse 7

*Jesus has purchased the bride/church.

A. <u>The Compassion for the Church</u>

"Husbands, love your wives, even as Christ also loved the church the church and gave himself for it."

Ephesians 5:25 KJV

*Jesus loves the church.

*We should love the things that Jesus loves.

1. We should be Dedicated to It
2. We should be Devoted to It

*We should love the things that Jesus loves.

*It is a great privilege to be a church member.

"Not forsaking the assembling of ourselves together as the manner of some is; but exhorting one another: and so much the more, as ye see the day approaching."

Hebrews 10:25 KJV

1. Pray for Your Church
2. Participate in Your Church
3. Promote Your Church

B. <u>The Cost of the Church</u>

*Jesus gave His life in order to purchase the church.

"Husbands, love your wives, even as Christ also loved the church, and gave himself for it." **Ephesians 5:25 KJV**

*Jesus paid the ultimate price by giving His life.

"For ye are bought with a price: therefore glorify God in your body, and in your spirit, which are God's."

1 Corinthians 6:20 KJV

89

II. THE PURIFICATION OF THE BRIDE – verses 7, 8 –
"Made Herself Ready"

*The Church is going to be purified and perfected.

*This purification and perfection process will take place at the **Judgment Seat of Christ**

"For we must all appear before the judgment seat of Christ; that every one may receive the things done in his body, according to that he hath done, whether good or bad."
2 Corinthians 5:10 KJV

"But why do you judge your brother? Or why do you show contempt for your brother? For we shall all stand before the judgment seat of Christ." **Romans 14:10 NKJV**

*How has she been purified?

A. She Has Been Cleansed

*The agent of our cleansing is the blood of Jesus.

*The blood of Jesus Christ washes our sins away.

"In whom we have redemption through his blood, the forgiveness of sins, according to the riches of his grace."
Ephesians 1:7 KJV

B. She Had Been Clothed – *"Fine Linen"*

*Wedding garments are important.

*Parable of the Wedding in Matthew 22:1-14

*We are unrighteous because of sin (Isaiah 64:6), but we are made righteous in Jesus Christ (2 Corinthians 5:21).

*Our wedding garment is the righteousness of Christ.

"And be found in him, not having mine own righteousness, which is of the law, but that which is through the faith of Christ, the righteousness which is of God by faith."
Philippians 3:9 KJV

"I will greatly rejoice in the Lord, my soul shall be joyful in my God; for he hath clothed me with the garments of salvation, he hath covered me with the robe of righteousness, as a bridegroom decketh himself with ornaments, and as a bride adorneth herself with her jewels." **Isaiah 61:10 KJV**

III. THE PRESENTATION OF THE BRIDE – verse 7

*At the Marriage Supper of the Lamb, the church will be presented to Jesus.

"For I am jealous over you with godly jealously: for I have espoused you to one husband, that I may present you as a chaste virgin to Christ." **2 Corinthians 11:2 KJV**

*The Marriage Supper of the Lamb will be a . . .

A. <u>Time of Celebration</u>

*God intends for His people to be joyful.

*Weddings are a joyful occasion.

"These things have I spoken unto you, that my joy might remain in you; and that your joy, might be full."
John 15:11 KJV

"Behold, God is my salvation; I will trust, and not be afraid: for the Lord Jehovah is my strength and my song; he also is become my salvation. Therefore with joy shall ye draw water out of the wells of salvation."
Isaiah 12:2, 3 KJV

"In the Rapture Jesus will catch us up, at the Judgment Seat He will clean us up, and at the Marriage Supper He will cheer us up!" **Dr. Jerry Vines**[88]

B. <u>Time of Communion</u>

*The Marriage Supper of the Lamb will unite us with Christ in perfect harmony and oneness.

*God wants us to know Him in a personal and intimate way.

"That which we have seen and heard declare we unto you, that ye also may have fellowship with us: and truly our fellowship is with the Father, and with his Son Jesus Christ." **1 John 1:3 KJV**

*You can commune and fellowship with God on a daily basis.

"And this is life, eternal, that they might know thee the only true God, and Jesus Christ whom thou hast sent."
John 17:3 KJV

CONCLUSION

*In order to come to the Marriage Supper of the Lamb, you must answer the invitation – verse 9

*Jesus calls and personally invites you to come.
"And the Spirit and the bride say, Come. And let him that heareth say, Come. And let him that is athirst come. And whosoever will, let him take the water of life freely." **Revelation 22:17 KJV**

> *"Softly and tenderly Jesus is calling,*
> *Calling for you and for me;*
> *See, on the portals He's waiting and watching,*
> *Watching for you and for me.*
> *Come home, come home,*
> *Ye who are weary come home;*
> *Earnestly, tenderly, Jesus is calling,*
> *Calling, O sinner come home!"*
> **Will L. Thompson**[89]

"THE GLORIOUS RETURN"
Revelation 19:11-21

*At the end of the Tribulation Period the Lord Jesus is going to return to this earth in a glorious manner.
*He will return to this earth with majesty and power.
*The Glorious Return is what we refer to as the Second Coming.
*The following chart helps to explain the differences between the Rapture of the Church in the air and the Glorious Return of Christ (Second Coming) on earth.

RAPTURE 1 Thessalonians 4:16-18	GLORIOUS RETURN Revelation 19:11-21
"Thief in the Night" 2 Peter 3:10	*"Every Eye Shall See Him"* Revelation 1:7
Returns in the Air (Clouds) 1 Thessalonians 4:17	Returns to Earth (Mount of Olives) Zechariah 14:4
Comes to Claim His Bride (Believers) John 14:3	Comes to Judge the Earth (The Wicked) Revelation 19:11
Beginning of the Tribulational Period Revelation 4:1	End of the Tribulational Period Revelation 22:11

*The *"Glorious Return"* of Christ to the Mount of Olives is explained in great detail in Revelation 19:11-21.

*There are several important truths to consider related to this important eschatological event.

I. THE COMING OF CHRIST

*Jesus appears with great

A. <u>Authority</u>

*He is riding a white horse (verse 11).

*White is symbolic of His purity (verse 13). The first time Jesus rode into Jerusalem from the Mount of Olives, He rode a donkey (Mark 11:1-10). The donkey is a symbol of peace. However, when He appears in His *"Glorious Return"* He will be riding a white horse. The horse is symbolic of strength and power. The second time He descends from the Mount of Olives He will come to *"make war"* in righteousness (verse 11).

*Several titles are given to Jesus in this passage that also refer to His authority.

1. *"Faithful"* (verse 11),
2. *"True"* (verse 11)
3. *"The Word of God"* (verse 13)

*Verse 15 also describes Him having a *"sharp sword"* coming out of His mouth.

This is another reference to the authority of the Word of God.

"For the word of God is living and powerful, and sharper than any two-edged sword, piercing even to the division of soul and spirit, and of joints and marrow, and is a discerner of the thoughts and intents of the heart."
Hebrews 4:12 NKJV

B. <u>Majesty</u>

*Christ's majesty and royalty are revealed in his crowns (verse 12) and his title of *"KING OF KINGS, AND LORD OF LORDS"* (verse 16).

*He will return as a conquering King with vengeance and wrath (verse 11).

*When the angel, Gabriel, appeared to the Virgin Mary, he referred to the future kingdom of Christ.

"And behold, you will conceive in your womb and bring forth a Son, and shall call His name JESUS. He will be great, and will be called the Son of the Highest: and the Lord God will give Him the throne of His father David. And He will reign over the house of Jacob forever; and of His kingdom there will be no end."
Luke 1:31-33 NKJV

II. THE COMPANIONS OF CHRIST

"And the armies in heaven, clothed in fine linen, white and clean, followed Him on white horses."
Revelation 19:14 NKJV

A. Their Citizenship

*Those who accompany Jesus Christ are the saints of God and citizens of heaven.

*Heaven is the residence for all Christians.

"For our citizenship is in heaven, from which we also eagerly wait for the Savior, the Lord Jesus Christ."
Philippians 3:20 NKJV

B. Their Cleanliness

*Their attire is described as white and clean and they are riding on white horses.

*This is a reference to their purity.

*In Christ Jesus we are made clean and righteous.

"Come now, and let us reason together, saith the Lord: though your sins be as scarlet, they shall be as white as snow; though they be red like crimson, they shall be as wool." **Isaiah 1:18 KJV**

"And such were some of you. But you were washed, you were sanctified, you were justified in the name of the Lord Jesus Christ and by the Spirit of God."
1 Corinthians 6:11 ESV

*Dr. David Jeremiah in his book, *What in the World is Going On?*, writes the following:

These legions are dressed not in military fatigues but in dazzling white. Yet they need not worry about their

94

pristine uniforms getting soiled because their role is largely ceremonial and honorary; they will not fight. Jesus Himself will slay the rebels with the deadly sword darting out of His mouth.[90]

III. THE CONQUEST OF CHRIST

*The awesomeness of Christ is revealed in His vengeance and wrath.

*Revelation 19:11 says He comes to *"judge and make war."* Revelation 19:12 declares *"His eyes were as a flame of fire."*

*Jesus comes to liberate Jerusalem and defeat the Antichrist at the Battle of Armageddon.

"And he gathered them together into a place called in the Hebrew tongue Armageddon." **Revelation 16:16 KJV** *"Armageddon"* is the Hebrew name for Mt. Megiddo.[91]

*Mt. Megiddo overlooks the Valley of Jezreel.

*Napoleon described this valley as the greatest battlefield that he had ever seen.[92]

*Mark Hitchcock in his book, *The End*, writes the following about this climatic battle.

Jesus will crush the gathered horde at Armageddon who is under the authority of the Antichrist. In a futile, foolish show of bravado, the assembled armies will turn against Christ as He descends from heaven. In the briefest battle in history, the King of kings and Lord of lords will prevail effortlessly.[93]

*At the Battle of Armageddon Jesus will conquer
1. The Antichrist (verse 20)
2. The False Prophet (verse 20)
3. Wicked sinners (verse 21

*The conquest and judgment of Jesus will be

A. <u>Swift</u>
B. <u>Severe</u>
C. <u>Sure</u> **(final and complete)**

*So massive and great will be the destruction at His conquest that the fowls (vultures and buzzards) of the air will be summoned to eat the flesh of the dead (verses 17, 18).

95

*The *"Glorious Return"* of Jesus will mark the end of the Tribulation Period and usher in the Millennial Reign of Christ upon the earth (Revelation 20:1-6).

"The Coming Kingdom"

"His Kingdom is coming!
Oh, tell me the story!
God's banner exalted shall be;
The earth shall be filled
with His wonder and glory,
As the waters that cover the sea."[94]

"THE MILLENNIAL REIGN OF CHRIST"
Revelation 20:1-6

"Millennium" – Latin word that means 1,000 years.

*The 1,000 is referred to six times in this chapter (verses 2, 3, 4, 5, 6, 7).

*There are three main views concerning the millennial reign of Jesus Christ.

1. **Postmillennialism**
   *Christ does not return until the 1,000 years are over.
   *Man keeps getting better and improving until Christ returns.
   *Optimistic view at the beginning of the 20th Century.
   *W. W. I. and W. W. II. devastated this view.

2. **Amillennialism**
   *Spiritualizes the 1,000 years.
   *The 1,000 years are symbolic.
   *Actually, a NON-millennialist.

3. **Premillennialism**
   *Revelation 20 must be interpreted literally.
   *The Millennial Reign will be an ideal world.
   *Perfect world – Like the world of Adam and Eve in the Garden of Eden.
   *He will reign with Christ as He intended for His people to do in the beginning of time.
   *The following are some words that describe the Millennium.

1. Wonderful
2. Peaceful
3. Joyful
4. Beautiful
5. Delightful

*Dr. Adrian Rogers describes the Millennial Kingdom
as follows:

> Imagine a time when there will be no more poverty and
> every person will have all that his heart desires. Imagine that,
> and more. There will be no prisons, no hospitals, no mental
> institutions, no army bases, no gambling dens, and no houses
> of prostitution. The bloom of youth will be on everyone's
> cheek. The wolf and the lamb, the calf and the lion, and the
> little child and the serpent will all play together. The
> implements of war will be relics of the past. Israel will be
> restored to her land. Jerusalem will be the world's capital.
> The resurrected saints will rule and reign with the Lord Jesus
> Christ. The desert will blossom like a rose, and the earth will
> be filled with the knowledge of the glory of the Lord as
> waters that cover the sea. The time will be called the Golden
> Age (or the millennium of Christ's reign on earth).[95]

*Read Isaiah 35:1-10 for a description of the Millennial Kingdom.
*Note the following concerning the Millennial Reign of
Christ:

I. THE REMOVAL OF SATAN – verses 1-3
*Satan will be removed during the Millennial Reign of Christ.
*As a result, the world will be free from the following:

A. Free from Satan's Aim
*His aim is to kill, steal, and destroy.
"The thief cometh not, but for to steal, and to kill, and to
destroy . . . ." **John 10:10 KJV**
*He wants to destroy lives, families, churches, and nations.

B. Free from Satan's Attacks
*Spiritual warfare will not be present in the Millennial
Kingdom.

"Be sober, be vigilant; because your adversary the devil, as a roaring lion, walketh about seeking whom he may devour." **1 Peter 5:8 KJV**

C. **Free from Satan's Ammunition**

  *His ammunition and tactics are referred to in a number of ways in the Bible.

  1. Devices – 2 Corinthians 2:11
  2. Tricks – Ephesians 6:11
  3. Snares – 2 Timothy 2:26
  4. Enticements – James 1:14-16

II. THE REIGN OF THE SAVIOR – verses 4, 6

  *Jesus Christ will rule and reign during the Millennial Kingdom.

  *He will be in control.

  *There are several forms of government.

  1. Monarchy – King or Queen Rules
  2. Dictatorship – One person rules
  3. Democracy – People rule through a Republic
  4. Theocracy – God rules.

    *God will rule during the Millennium.

A. **The Supremacy of His Rule**

  *There have been many rulers throughout history.

  *Some good and some bad.

  *Jesus will outshine them all.

  "I saw in the night visions, and, behold, one like the Son of man came with the clouds of heaven, and came to the Ancient of days, and they brought him near before him. And there was given him dominion, and glory, and a kingdom, that all people, nations, and languages, should serve him: his dominion is an everlasting dominion, which shall not pass away, and his kingdom that which shall not be destroyed." **Daniel 7:13, 14 KJV**

  "Behold, the days come, saith the Lord, that I will raise unto David a righteous Branch, and a King shall reign and prosper, and shall execute judgment and justice in the earth." **Jeremiah 23:6 KJV**

B. **The Seat of His Rule**

  *Jesus will reign from the city of Jerusalem.

98

"The word that Isaiah the son of Amoz saw concerning
Judah and Jerusalem. And it shall come to pass in the last
days, that the mountain of the Lord's house shall be
established in the top of the mountains, and shall be
exalted above the hills; and all nations shall flow unto it.
And many people shall go and say, Come ye, and let us go
up to the mountain of the Lord, to the house of the God of
Jacob; and he will teach us of his ways, and we will walk
in his paths; for out of Zion shall go forth the law, and the
word of the Lord from Jerusalem." **Isaiah 2:1-3 KJV**

III. THE REBIRTH OF SOCIETY
*Society will be reestablished and reborn.
*This new society will be marked in two unique ways.
A. It will be a Peaceful Society
*It will be a society of harmony and peace because the
Prince of Peace will rule.
"And he shall judge among the nations, and shall rebuke
many people: and they shall beat their swords into
plowshares, and their spears into pruninghooks: nation
shall not lift up sword against nation, neither shall they
learn war any more." **Isaiah 2:4 KJV**
"And all thy children shall be taught of the Lord; and great
shall be the peace of thy children." **Isaiah 54:13 KJV**
*There will be peace in the animal kingdom as well.
"The wolf will live with the lamb, the leopard will lie down
with the goat, the calf and the lion and the yearling
together; and a little child will lead them. The cow will
feed with the bear, their young will lie down together, and
the lion will eat straw like the ox. The infant will play near
the hold of the cobra, and the young child put his hand into
the viper's nest. They will neither harm nor destroy on all
my holy mountain, for the earth will be full of the
knowledge of the Lord as the waters cover the sea."
Isaiah 11:6-9 NIV
B. It will be a Perfect Society
*The earth was cursed as a result of sin in the Garden of
Eden (Genesis 3:17, 18).
*The curse will be removed during the Millennial reign.

*Romans 8:19-21 describes the removal of this curse.
"For the earnest expectation of the creature waiteth for the manifestation of the sons of God. For the creature was made subject to vanity, not willing, but by reason of him who had subjected the same in hope, Because the creature itself also shall be delivered from the bondage of corruption into the glorious liberty of the children of God."
Romans 8:19-21 KJV
*Isaiah 35:9 states, ". . . the redeemed shall walk there."
*The way to experience the Millennial Kingdom is to be redeemed.
*In order to be redeemed you must come to the **REDEEMER!!**
*Jesus Christ is our **REDEEMER!!**
"For you know that it was not with perishable things such as silver or gold that you were redeemed from the empty way of life handed down to you from your forefathers, but with the precious blood of Christ, a lamb without blemish or defect." **1 Peter 1:18, 19 NIV**

"Redeemed, how I love to proclaim it!
Redeemed by the blood of the Lamb;
Redeemed thro' His infinite mercy,
His child, and forever, I am."
Fanny J. Crosby[96]

"SATAN'S LAST STAND"
Revelation 20:7-10
*This passage reveals the final destiny of Satan.
*This will be the final chapter in the history of Satan.
*God is greater and more powerful than Satan.

I. HIS DELIVERANCE – verse 7
*Satan is released from the bottomless pit.
*This is necessary for him to face his final destiny.

II. HIS DECEPTION – verse 8
"The naming of 'Gog and Magog' (verse 8) does not equate this battle with the one described in Ezekiel 38-39; for that army invades from the north, while this one comes from the four corners of the earth." **Warren W. Wiersbe**[97]

*Satan will deceive the many that were born during the Millennium.

*This event reminds us of two things:

A. The Condition of the Heart

    *A perfect environment does not produce a perfect heart.

    *The human heart is prone to sin.

    "The heart is deceitful above all things, and desperately wicked: who can know it?" **Jeremiah 17:9 KJV**

B. The Cure for the Heart

    *Humanity does not need reformation but transformation.

    *Only Christ can change a heart.

    "Therefore if anyone is in Christ, the new creation has come: The old has gone, the new is here!"

                2 Corinthians 5:17 NIV

III. HIS DEFEAT – verse 9

    *The forces of evil are no match for the power of God.

    A. It will be Fierce

    B. It will be Firey

    C. It will be Final

IV. HIS DESTINY – verse 10

    A. The Place – *"lake of fire"*

    B. The Punishment – *"tormented day and night"*

    C. The Permanence – *"for ever and ever"*

    *Satan's final destiny is the *"lake of fire."*

"And tho' this world with devils filled,
Should threaten to undo us,
We will not fear,
For God hath willed His truth
To triumph thro' us:
The Prince of Darkness grim,
We tremble not for him;
His rage we can endure,
For lo, his doom is sure,
One little word shall fell him."
Martin Luther[98]

"THE GREAT WHITE THRONE JUDGMENT"
Revelation 20:11-15

*Court Room dramas are a popular theme on television and in the movies.

*At the conclusion of the Millennial Reign of Christ there will be a time of judgment for Satan and Sinners.

*Revelation 20:11-15 reveal the courtroom of God.

I. THE PERSON ON THE THRONE – verses 11, 12

*The Person on the throne is God Himself.

*Almighty God is the supreme judge of the universe.

*God is a God of love, but He is also a God of judgment.

"The Lord is known by the judgment which he executeth."
Psalm 9:16 KJV

*He is a fair judge.

"Before the Lord: for he cometh, for he cometh to judge the earth: he shall judge the world with righteousness, and the people with his truth." **Psalm 96:13 KJV**

*Note the following:

A. His Awesomeness – verse 11

*God's presence is awesome.

"It is a fearful thing to fall into the hands of the living God."
Hebrews 10:31 KJV

B. His Attributes

1. He is Holy

"Ye shall therefore be holy, for I am holy."
Leviticus 11:45 KJV

2. He is Righteous

"The Lord is righteous in all his ways, and holy in all his works." **Psalm 145:17 KJV**

3. He is Just

"He is the Rock, his work is perfect: for all his ways are judgment: a God of truth and without iniquity, just and right is he." **Deuteronomy 32:4 KJV**

4. He is Powerful

"God hath spoken once; twice have I heard this; that power belongeth unto God." **Psalm 62:11 KJV**

II. THE PEOPLE AT THE THRONE – verse 12 – *"Dead"*

"Dead" – unsaved, lost, unbelieving

*Used four times in this passage.

*Apart from Christ a person is spiritually dead.

"For the wages of sin is death . . . ." **Romans 6:23 KJV**

"And you hath he quickened who were dead in trespasses and sins." **Ephesians 2:1 KJV**

"And you, being dead in your sins and the uncircumcision of your flesh, hath he quickened together with him, having forgiven you all trespasses." **Colossians 2:13 KJV**

A. The Impartiality of this Judgment – verse 12

"Small and great"

*When a person stands before God at the Great White Throne Judgment, prestige, position, prominence, and popularity will have no bearing or influence.

*All lost people will stand before God at the Great White Throne.

1. Out and Out Sinner

"The wicked shall be turned into hell, and all the nations that forget God." **Psalm 9:17 KJV**

2. Self-Righteous

". . . For everyone that exalteth himself shall be abased and he that humbleth himself shall be exalted."

Luke 18:14 KJV

3. Procrastinators

"Behold, now is the accepted time; behold, now is the day of salvation." **2 Corinthians 6:2 KJV**

B. The Inescapability of this Judgment-vss. 11, 13

*No one will escape this judgment.

"And as it is appointed unto men once to die, but after this the judgment." **Hebrews 9:27 KJV**

III. THE PROCEDURE AT THE THRONE – verse 12

"The Books were opened"

*These books reveal the evidence that sentences the lost to Hell.

*It is evidence that convicts or frees.

*Four reasons why this evidence is important.

A. <u>To Reveal that Works Cannot Save</u>
"For by grace are ye saved through faith, and that not of yourselves: it is the gift of God: not of works, lest any man should boast." **Ephesians 2:8, 9 KJV**

B. <u>To Determine their Degree of Punishment in Hell</u> – **verse 13**
"Who will render to every man according to his deeds: in the day when God shall judge the secrets of men by Jesus Christ according to my gospel." **Romans 2:6, 16 KJV**
*The great Bible expositor, Warren Wiersbe, helps us to understand this truth.

> Why, then, will Jesus Christ consider the works, good and bad, of the people before the white throne? To determine the degree of punishment they will endure in hell. All of these people will be cast into hell. Their personal rejection of Jesus Christ has already determined their destiny. But Jesus Christ is a righteous Judge, and He will assign each sinner the place that he deserves. There are degrees of punishment in hell (Matthew 11:20-24). Each lost sinner will receive just what is due him, and none will be able to argue with the Lord or question His decision. God knows what sinners are doing, and His books will reveal the truth.
> **Warren W. Wiersbe**[99]

C. <u>To Reveal What Sent them There</u> – **vss. 12, 15**
*There names are not written in the Book of Life.
*The sin of rejection has sent them to Hell.

D. <u>To Reveal that They have been Treated Fairly</u> **– verse 12**
*We have a fair and just God!
*He is righteous.

IV. THE PUNISHMENT AT THE THRONE – vs. 15
*The punishment for the lost is the Lake of Fire.
*The Lake of Fire can be described in three ways.

A. **A Place of Suffering**
"And these shall go away into everlasting punishment: but the righteous into life eternal." **Matthew 25:46 KJV**

B. **A Place of Separation**
"But the children of the kingdom shall be cast out into outer darkness: there shall be weeping and gnashing of teeth." **Matthew 8:12 KJV**

C. **A Place of Sorrow**
"But Abraham said, Son, remember that thou in thy lifetime receivedst thy good things, and likewise Lazarus evil things: but now he is comforted, and thou art tormented." **Luke 16:25**

*A person does not have to be sentenced to Hell.

*God never intended for any person to live in Hell.

*Individuals send themselves to Hell when they reject Jesus Christ as their Lord and Savior.

*Hell was prepared for the Devil and his angels.

"Then shall he say also unto them on the left hand, depart from me, ye cursed, into everlasting fire, prepared for the Devil and his angels." **Matthew 25:41**

READ JOHN 3:18, 36

"Come, ye sinners, poor and needy,
Weak and wounded, sick and sore;
Jesus ready stands to save you,
Full of pity, love, and pow'r."
Joseph Hart[100]

"OUR HEAVENLY HOME"
Revelation 21:1-4

*As Christians our eternal home is in Heaven.

*Abraham understood this reality.

"For he looked for a city which hath foundations, whose builder and maker is God." **Hebrews 11:10 KJV**

"But our citizenship is in heaven, and from it we await a Savior, the Lord Jesus Christ." **Philippians 3:20 ESV**

*Note the following about Heaven in this passage.

I. HEAVEN IS A REAL PLACE
*Heaven is not a fairy tale or a fable.
*Heaven is a promised place.
A. **Promised by the Word of God**
*Job understood that Heaven is real.
"And though after my skin worms destroy this body, yet in my flesh shall I see God." **Job 19:26 KJV**
"Thou shalt guide me with thy counsel, and afterward receive me to glory." **Psalm 73:24 KJV**
B. **Promised by the Son of God**
*Jesus gave the promise of Heaven to His disciples.
"In my Father's house are many mansions: if it were not so, I would have told you, I go to prepare a place for you."
John 14:6 KJV
*Jesus told the thief on the cross.
"Verily I say unto thee, To day shalt thou be with me in paradise." **Luke 23:43 KJV**

"There's a land that is fairer than day,
And by faith we can see it afar;
For the Father waits over the way
To prepare us a dwelling place there.
In the Sweet by and by,
We shall meet on that beautiful shore;
In the Sweet by and by,
We shall meet on that beautiful shore."
Samford F. Bennett[101]

II. HEAVEN IS A REMARKABLE PLACE
". . . Eye hath not seen, nor ear heard, neither have entered into the heart of man, the things which God hath prepared for them that love him." **1 Corinthians 2:9 KJV**
*Heaven is a glorious and beautiful place.
*It is beautiful in . . .
1. *Appearance* – **Revelation 21:11**
*She is described as a *"bride"* – Revelation 21:2, 9
2. *Architecture* – **Revelation 21:12-14, 18-21**

106

*What makes Heaven a remarkable place?

A. <u>It is a Prepared Place</u>

*Heaven is conceived, designed, and constructed by the great Architect of the Universe.

"And if I go and *prepare* a place for you, I will come again, and receive you unto myself; that where I am, there ye may be also." **John 14:3 KJV**

"Instead, they were longing for a better country-a heavenly one. Therefore God is not ashamed to be called their God, for he has *prepared* a city for them." **Hebrews 11:16 NIV**

". . . Eye hath not seen, nor ear heard, neither have entered into the heart of man, the things which God hath *prepared* for them that love him." **1 Corinthians 2:9 KJV**

B. <u>Heaven is a Personal Place</u> – Revelation 21:3;
                                        Revelation 22:4

*We will be in the presence of God.

*We will walk and commune with Him for all of eternity.

"And if I go and prepare a place for you, I will come again, and receive you unto myself; *that where I am, there ye may be also."* **John 14:3 KJV**

"We are confident, I say, and would prefer to be away from the body and at home with the Lord."
                        2 Corinthians 5:8 NIV

"For to me to live is Christ, and to die is gain. For I am in a strait betwixt two, having a desire to depart, and to be with Christ, which is far better." **Philippians 1:21, 23 KJV**

"Face to face with Christ, my Savior,
Face to face – what will it be,
When with rapture I behold Him,
Jesus Christ who died for me?
Face to face I shall behold Him,
Far beyond the starry sky;
Face to face in all His glory,
I shall see Him by and by!"
Carrie E. Breck[102]

107

C. <u>Heaven is a Permanent Place</u> – Revelation 22:5
  *Heaven is eternal – earth is temporary.
  *Homes on earth can be destroyed by fire, tornado,
    hurricane, flood, etc.
  *Our home in Heaven can never be destroyed.
  "For we know that if our earthly house, a tent, is destroyed,
    we have a building from God, a house not made with
    hands, eternal in the heavens."
            2 Corinthians 5:1 HCSB
D. <u>Heaven is a Perfect Place</u> – Revelation 21:16
  *The city of Heaven is a perfect cube – *"Foursquare"*
  *Heaven is perfect in every dimension.
  "Be ye therefore perfect, even as your Father which is in
    Heaven is perfect." **Matthew 5:48 KJV**
  1. No Shortcomings in Heaven
  2. No Sin in Heaven
      *Revelation 22:3 – *"No More Curse"*
  3. No Satan in Heaven
E. <u>Heaven is a Painless Place</u> – Revelation 21:4
  1. No Sorrow in Heaven
  2. No Sickness in Heaven
  3. No Suffering in Heaven
  4. No Separation in Heaven
  5. No Sadness in Heaven
F. <u>Heaven is a Plentiful Place</u>
  *All of our needs will be met in Heaven.
  1. Plentiful in Food – Revelation 22:2
  2. Plentiful in Water – Revelation 21:6, 22:1

III. **HEAVEN IS A RESERVED PLACE** – Revelation 21:27
  *Heaven is a prepared place for prepared people.
  *Only Christians go to Heaven.
  *Our reservations are recorded in the *"Lamb's Book of Life"*
  *Jesus is the only way to Heaven.
  "Enter ye in at the strait gate: for wide is the gate, and broad is
    the way, that leadeth to destruction, and many there be which
    go in thereat: Because strait is the gate, and narrow is the
    way, which leadeth unto life, and few there be that find it."
            Matthew 7:13, 14 KJV

"I am the way, the truth, and the life: no man cometh unto the Father but by me." **John 14:6 KJV**

*How do you get into the *"Lamb's Book of Life"*

A. Acknowledge Christ

*Realize that Christ is the only way of salvation.

"That if thou shalt confess with thy mouth the Lord Jesus, and shalt believe in thine heart that God hath raised him from the dead, thou shalt be saved. For with the heart man believeth unto righteousness, and with the mouth confession is made unto salvation."

Romans 10:9, 10 KJV

B. Accept Christ

"For whosever shall call upon the name of the Lord shall be saved." **Romans 10:13 KJV**

"Behold, I stand at the door, and knock: if any man hear my voice, and open the door, I will come in to him, and will sup with him, and he with me."

Revelation 3:20 KJV

***TO BE HEAVEN BOUND, YOU MUST BE HEAVEN BORN!**

"When the trumpet of the Lord shall sound,
And time shall be no more,
And the morning breaks,
eternal, bright, and fair;
When the saved of earth shall gather
over on the other shore,
And the roll is call up yonder,
I'll be there."
James M. Black[103]

"FINAL WORDS"
Revelation 22:6-21

*In these verses we find the final words of Jesus.
*Note the following:

I. THE CERTAINTY – verses 7, 12, 20
   A. Anticipation of His Coming

*Jesus is coming back *"quickly."*
*The idea is imminence.
*Jesus' coming could happen any moment.
"Looking for that blessed hope, and the glorious
   appearing of the great God and our Savior Jesus Christ."
                    Titus 2:13 KJV
B. <u>Preparation for His Coming</u> – verse 7 –
                              "keepeth"
*We must be ready for His arrival.
"Teaching us that, denying ungodliness and worldly lusts,
   we should live soberly, righteously, and godly, in this
   present world." **Titus 2:12 KJV**
"Therefore be ye also ready: for in such an hour as ye
   think not the Son of man cometh."
                    Matthew 24:44 KJV

II. THE COMMAND – verses 8, 9
*The command is that we are to *"worship God."*
"O worship the Lord in the beauty of holiness: fear before
   him, all the earth." **Psalm 96:9 KJV**
*Worship God . . .
A. <u>Reverently</u>
B. <u>Passionately</u>
C. <u>Constantly</u>
D. <u>Sincerely</u>
   "God is a Spirit: and they that worship him must worship
   him in spirit and in truth." **John 4:24**

III. THE CHALLENGE – verses 10, 11
*The challenge is to live a life that honors God.
*There will not be time to change or make corrections at the
   coming of Christ.
A. <u>Be Faithful to God</u>
B. <u>Be Focused on God</u>
C. <u>Be Fruitful for God</u> – Live a productive life.

IV. THE CONFESSION – verses 12, 16
*Jesus confesses that He is the

A. *"Alpha and Omega"* - verse 12
*Revelation opens with this confession and
closing with it. See Revelation 1:8
B. *"Bright and Morning Star"* - verse 16

"This is the brightest star announcing the arrival of the
day. When Jesus comes, he will be the brightest star
who will shatter the darkness of man's night and herald
the dawn of God's glorious day." **John MacArthur**[104]

V. THE COMFORT – verse 14
*The comfort is . . .
A. Entrance into Heaven – *"enter in through the
gates of the city"*
B. Enjoyments of Heaven – *"tree of life"*

VI. THE CONTRAST – verse 15
*Note their . . .
A. Exclusion – *"without"*
B. Evil Nature

VII. THE CONSOLATION – verse 17
*The encouragement is to come to Christ.
*The word, *"come,"* appears three times in this verse.
*This is a **personal** and a **universal** invitation.
*Come represents all who are invited.

C – hildren
O – lder Folks
M – iddle Aged
E – veryone

"Come unto me all ye that labor and are heavy laden, and I
will give you rest." **Matthew 11:28 KJV**

VIII. THE CAUTION – verses 18, 19
*The caution is not to tamper with God's Word.
*We have the complete revelation of God as He intends for us
to have.

*God's Word is not to be tampered with because it is . . .
A. **Inspired** – 2 Timothy 3:16, 2 Peter 1:21
B. **Truth** – John 8:31, 32; Psalm 119:160
C. **Eternal** – Psalm 119:89, Isaiah 40:8, Matthew 24:3
D. **Perfect** – Psalm 19:7

IX. **THE CHEER – verse 21**
*Cheer is found in the grace of God.
*God gives . . .
A. **Saving Grace** – Ephesians 2:8
B. **Sustaining Grace** – 2 Corinthians 1:9
C. **Special Grace** – 1 Corinthians 15:10
D. **Supernatural Grace** – Ephesians 4:7

"Amazing Grace! How sweet the sound,
That saved a wretch like me!
I once was lost, but am found,
Was blind, but now I see."
John Newton[105]

"I have read the last page of the Bible. It is all going to turn out all right." Billy Graham[106]

REFERENCES/ENDNOTES

[1]John MacArthur, *The MacArthur Bible Commentary* (Nashville: Thomas Nelson Publishers, 2005), 1989.

[2]*NIV Archaeological Study Bible* (Grand Rapids, Michigan: Zondervan Publishers, 2005), 2046. And Daniel Green in the *Moody Bible Commentary* (Chicago: Moody Press, 2014), 1999.

[3]Warren W. Wiersbe, *With the Word* (Nashville: Thomas Nelson Publishers, 1991), 846.

[4]John Walvoord, *The Revelation of Jesus Christ* (Chicago: Moody Press, 1966), 13-14.

[5]Lehman Strauss, *The Book of Revelation* (Neptune, New Jersey: Loizeaux Brothers, 1964), 17.

[6]Warren W. Wiersbe, *Expository Outlines on the New Testament* (Covington, Kentucky: Calvary Book Room, 1965), 471-474.

[7]John MacArthur, *The MacArthur Bible Commentary* (Nashville: Thomas Nelson Publishers, 2005), 2006.

[8]*The Believer's Study Bible* (Nashville: Thomas Nelson Publishers, 1991), 1888.

[9]Walter Chalmers Smith, *"Immortal, Invisible, God Only Wise,"* in The Baptist Hymnal (Nashville: Convention Press, 1991), 6.

[10]William MacDonald, *Believer's Bible Commentary* (Nashville: Thomas Nelson Publishers, 1995), 2355.

[11]*ESV Archaeology Study Bible* (Wheaton, Illinois: Crossway, 2017), 1747.

[12]John D. Davis, *The Westminster Dictionary of the Bible* (Philadelphia: The Westminster Press, 1944), 167.

[13]Paul J. Achtemeier, ed., *The HarperCollins Bible Dictionary* (San Francisco: HarperCollins Publishers, 1985), 298.

[14]John D. Davis, *The Westminster Dictionary of the Bible* (Philadelphia: The Westminster Press, 1944), 167.

[15]Charles Caldwell Ryrie, *The Ryrie Study Bible* (Chicago: Moody Press, 2011), 1551.

[16]William R. Featherson, *"My Jesus, I Love Thee,"* in *The Baptist Hymnal* (Nashville: Convention Press, 1991), 211.

[17]Merrill C. Tenny, ed., *Pictorial Bible Dictionary* (Nashville: The Southwestern Company, 1975), 799.

[18]Ibid.

[19]Lehman Strauss, *The Book of Revelation* (Neptune, New Jersey: Loizeaux Brothers, 1964), 41.

[20]Ibid., 43.

[21]Matthew Bridges, *"Crown Him with Many Crowns,"* in *The Baptist Hymnal* (Nashville: Convention Press, 1991), 161.

[22]Merrill C. Tenny, ed., *Pictorial Bible Dictionary* (Nashville: The Southwestern Company, 1975), 636.

[23]John D. Davis, *The Westminster Dictionary of the Bible* (Philadelphia: The Westminster Press, 1944), 471.

[24]Merrill C. Tenny, ed., *Pictorial Bible Dictionary* (Nashville: The Southwestern Company, 1975), 637.

[25]Ibid.

[26]Lehman Strauss, *The Book of Revelation* (Neptune, New Jersey: Loizeaux Brothers, 1964), 48.

[27]George Duffield, Jr., *"Stand Up, Stand Up for Jesus,"* in *The Baptist Hymnal* (Nashville: Convention Press, 1991), 485.

[28]Lehman Strauss, *The Book of Revelation* (Neptune, New Jersey: Loizeaux Brothers, 1964), 58.

[29]B. B. McKinney, *"Serve the Lord with Gladness,"* in *The Baptist Hymnal* (Nashville: Convention Press, 1991), 495.

[30]Warren W. Wiersbe, *Be Victorious* (Wheaton, Illinois: Victor Books, 1986), 36, 37.

[31]B. B. McKinney, *"Send a Great Revival,"* in *The Baptist Hymnal* (Nashville: Convention Press, 1991), 466.

[32]Warren W. Wiersbe, *Be Victorious* (Wheaton, Illinois: Victor Books, 1986), 40.

[33]Lehman Strauss, *The Book of Revelation* (Neptune, New Jersey: Loizeaux Brothers, 1964), 78.

[34]Ibid., 80.

[35]Otis Skillings, *"The Bond of Love,"* in *The Baptist Hymnal* (Nashville: Convention Press, 1991), 384.

[36]John D. Davis and Henry Snyder Gehman, *The Westminster Dictionary of the Bible* (Philadelphia: The Westminster Press, 1944), 351.

[37]Lehman Strauss, *The Book of Revelation* (Neptune, New Jersey: Loizeaux Brothers, 1964), 93.

[38]Merrill C. Tenny, ed., *Pictorial Bible Dictionary* (Nashville: The Southwestern Company, 1975), 476.

[39]Lehman Strauss, *The Book of Revelation* (Neptune, New Jersey: Loizeaux Brothers, 1964), 94.

[40]Ralph Carmichael, *"The Savior is Waiting,"* in *The Baptist Hymnal* (Nashville: Convention Press, 1991), 321.

[41]Gary Frazier, *Signs of the Coming of Christ* (Arlington, Texas, Discovery Ministries, 2004), 33.

[42]Warren W. Wiersbe, *The Bible Exposition Commentary*, vol. 2 (Wheaton, Illinois: Victor Books, 1989), 180-181.

[43]Dottie Rambo, *"We Shall Behold Him,"* in *The Baptist Hymnal* (Nashville: Convention Press, 1991), 196.

[44]Elizabeth Mills, *"We'll Work Till Jesus Comes,"* in *The Baptist Hymnal* (Nashville: Convention Press, 1991), 608.

[45]Carl A. Blackmore, *"Some Golden Daybreak,"* in *Favorite Hymns of Praise* (Chicago: Tabernacle Publishing Company, 1968), 495.

[46]John MacArthur, *The MacArthur Bible Commentary* (Nashville: Thomas Nelson Publishers, 2005), 2006

[47]Leila Naylor Morris, *"What If It Were Today?,"* in *The Baptist Hymnal* (Nashville: Convention Press, 1991), 195.

[48]Warren W. Wiersbe, *Be Victorious* (Wheaton, Illinois: Victor Books, 1986), 52.

[49]Thomas Ken, *"Praise God, from Whom All Blessings Flow,"* in *The Baptist Hymnal* (Nashville: Convention Press, 1991), 253.

[50]Sammy Tippit, *Worthy of Worship* (Chicago: Moody Press, 1989), 11.

[51]H. A. Ironside, *Revelation* (Neptune, New Jersey: Loizeau Brothers, 1982), 91.

[52]Warren W. Wiersbe, *Be Victorious* (Wheaton, Illinois: Victor Books, 1986), 56.

[53]Twila Paris, *"We will Glorify,"* in *The Baptist Hymnal* (Convention Press, 1991), 213.

[54]Warren Wiersbe, *Be Victorious* (Wheaton, Illinois: Victor Books, 64.

[55]Warren Wiersbe, *Be Victorious* (Wheaton, Illinois: Victor Books, 68.

[56]J. Vernon McGee, *Revelation, Volume II* (Pasadena, California: Thru the Bible Books, 1979), 67.

[57]John MacArthur, *The MacArthur Bible Commentary* (Nashville: Thomas Nelson Publishers, 2005), 2008.

[58]H. Ernest Nichol, *"We've a Story to Tell,"* in *The Baptist Hymnal* (Nashville: Convention Press, 1991), 586.

[59]*"This World is Not My Home"* in Alton H. Howard, ed. *Songs of Faith and Praise* (West Monroe, Louisiana: Howard Publishing Company, 1994), 957.

[60]Gaither, William and Gloria, *"The Family of God,"* in *Hymns for the Family of God* (Nashville: Paragon Associates, Inc., 1976), 543.

[61]Sanford Bennett, *"There is a Land that is Fairer Than Day,"* in *The Baptist Hymnal* (Nashville: Convention Press, 1991), 515.

[62]Daniel Green, *"Revelation"* in *The Moody Bible Commentary* (Chicago: Moody Press, 2014), 2011.

[63]Warren W. Wiersbe, *Be Victorious* (Wheaton, Illinois: Victor Books, 1986), 80.

[64]John MacArthur, *The MacArthur Bible Commentary* (Nashville: Thomas Nelson Publishers, 2005), 2010.

[65]Leila Naylor Morris, *"Let Jesus Come into Your Heart,"* in *The Baptist Hymnal* (Convention Press, 1991), 311.

[66]Warren W. Wiersbe, *Be Victorious* (Wheaton, Illinois: Victor Books, 1986), 87.

[67]John Burton, Sr., *"Holy Bible, Book Divine,"* in *The Baptist Hymnal* (Nashville: Convention Press, 1991), 260.

[68]John MacArthur, *The MacArthur Bible Commentary* (Nashville: Thomas Nelson Publishers, 2005), 2012.

[69]Frances R. Havergal, *"Take My Life, and Let It Be,"* in *The United Methodist Hymnal* (Nashville: The United Methodist Publishing House, 1989), 399.

[70]Graham Kendrick, *"Shine, Jesus, Shine"* in *This Far by Faith* (Minneapolis: Augsburg Fortress, 1999), 64, 65.

[71]Anonymous, *"Come, Thou Almighty King"* in *The United Methodist Hymnal* (Nashville: The United Methodist Publishing House, 1989), 61.

[72]John MacArthur, *The MacArthur Bible Commentary* (Nashville: Thomas Nelson Publishers, 2005), 2015.

[73]Alfred E. Mulder, *"God, the Father of Your People,"* in *The Baptist Hymnal* (Nashville: Convention Press, 1991), 382.

[74]Sabine Baring-Gould, *"Onward, Christian Soldiers"* in *The United Methodist Hymnal* (Nashville: The United Methodist Publishing House, 1989), 575.

[75]W. E. Vine, *An Expository Dictionary of New Testament Words* (Old Tappan, New Jersey: Fleming H. Revell Company, 1966), 61-62.

[76]David Jeremiah, *What in the World is Going On?* (Nashville: Thomas Nelson, 2008), 146-152.

[77]John MacArthur, *The MacArthur Bible Commentary* (Nashville: Thomas Nelson Publishers, 2005), 2017.

[78]Gary Frazier, *Signs of the Coming of Christ* (Arlington, Texas: Discovery Ministries, 2004), 150.

[79]John MacArthur, *The MacArthur Bible Commentary* (Nashville: Thomas Nelson Publishers, 2005), 2018.

[80]Edward Mote, *"The Solid Rock,"* in *The Baptist Hymnal* (Nashville: Convention Press, 1991), 406.

[81]H. Ernest Nichol, *"We've a Story to Tell to the Nations,"* in *The United Methodist Hymnal* (Nashville: The United Methodist Publishing House, 1989), 569.

[82]Julia Ward Howe, *"Mine Eyes Have Seen the Glory,"* in *The Baptist Hymnal* (Nashville: Convention Press, 1991), 633.

[83]Warren W. Wiersbe, *Be Victorious* (Wheaton, Illinois: Victor Books, 1986), 118-119.

[84]John MacArthur, *The MacArthur Bible Commentary* (Nashville: Thomas Nelson Publishers, 2005), 2028.

[85]Sabine Baring-Gould, *"Onward, Christian Soldiers"* in *The United Methodist Hymnal* (Nashville: The United Methodist Publishing House, 1989), 575.

[86]David Jeremiah, *The Jeremiah Study Bible* (Nashville: Worthy Publishing, 2013), 1861.

[87] *"We Shall Overcome,"* in *This Far by Faith* (Minneapolis: Augsburg Fortress, 1999), 213.

[88]Jerry Vines, *I Shall Return* (Wheaton, Illinois: Victor Books, 1979), 65.

[89]Will L. Thompson, *"Softly and Tenderly,"* in *The Baptist Hymnal* (Nashville: Convention Press, 1991), 312.

[90]David Jeremiah, *What in the World is Going On?* (Nashville: Thomas Nelson, 2008), 224.

[91]John MacArthur, *The MacArthur Bible Commentary* (Nashville: Thomas Nelson Publishers, 2005), 2026.

[92]Gary Frazier, *Signs of the Coming of Christ* (Arlington, Texas: Discovery Ministries, 2004), 192.

[93]Mark Hitchcock, *The End* (Carol Stream, Illinois: Tyndale House Publications, 2012), 387.

[94]Warren Wiersbe, *With the Word* (Nashville: Thomas Nelson Publishers, 1991), 861.

[95]Adrian Rogers, *Unveiling the End Times in our Time* (Nashville: Broadman and Holman Publishers, 2004), 240-241.

[96]Fanny J. Crosby, *"Redeemed, How I Love to Proclaim It,"* in *The Baptist Hymnal* (Nashville: Convention Press, 1991), 544.

[97]Warren W. Wiersbe, *Be Victorious* (Wheaton, Illinois: Victor Books, 1986), 141.

[98]Martin Luther, *"A Mighty Fortress is Our God,"* in *The Baptist Hymnal* (Nashville: Convention Press, 1991), 8.

[99]Warren W. Wiersbe, *Be Victorious* (Wheaton, Illinois: Victor Books, 1986), 143.

[100]Joseph Hart, *"Come, Ye Sinners, Poor and Needy,"* in *The Baptist Hymnal* (Nashville: Convention Press, 1991), 323.

[101]Samford F. Bennett, *"There's a Land That is Fairer Than Day,"* *The Baptist Hymnal* (Nashville: Convention Press, 1991), 515.

[102]Carrie E. Breck, *"Face to Face with Christ, My Savior,"* in *The Baptist Hymnal* (Nashville: Convention Press, 1991), 519.

[103]James M. Black, *"When the Roll is Called Up Yonder,"* in *The Baptist Hymnal* (Nashville: Convention Press, 1991), 516.

[104]John MacArthur, *The MacArthur Bible Commentary* (Nashville: Thomas Nelson Publishers, 2005), 2040.

[105]John Newton, *"Amazing Grace! How Sweet the Sound,"* in *The Baptist Hymnal* (Nashville: Convention Press, 1991), 330.

[106]Franklin Graham with Donna Lee Toney, *Billy Graham in Quotes*, (Nashville: Thomas Nelson Publishers, 2011), 48.

WORKS CITED AND CONSULTED

Achtemeier, Paul J., ed. *The HarperCollins Bible Dictionary*. San Francisco: HarperCollins Publishers, 1985.

Davis, John D. and Henry Snyder Gehman. *The Westminster Dictionary of the Bible*. Philadelphia: The Westminster Press, 1944.

ESV Archaeology Study Bible. Wheaton, Illinois: Crossway, 2017.

Favorite Hymns of Praise. Chicago: Tabernacle Publishing Company, 1968.

Frazier, Gary. *Signs of the Coming of Christ*. Arlington, Texas: Discovery Ministries, 2004.

Graham, Franklin with Donna Lee Toney. *Billy Graham in Quotes*. Nashville: Thomas Nelson Publishers, 2011.

Hitchcock, Mark. *The End*. Carol Stream, Illinois: Tyndale House Publications, 2012.

Howard, Alton H., ed. *Songs of Faith and Praise*. West Monroe, Louisiana: Howard Publishing Company, 1994.

Hymns for the Family of God. Nashville: Paragon Associates, Inc., 1976.

Jeremiah, David. *The Jeremiah Study Bible*. Nashville: Worthy Publishing, 2013.

Jeremiah, David. *The Prophecy Answer Book*. Nashville: Thomas Nelson Publishers, 2010.

Jeremiah, David. *What in the World is Going On?* Nashville: Thomas Nelson Publishers, 2008.

MacArthur, John. *The MacArthur Bible Commentary.* Nashville: Thomas Nelson Publishers, 2005.

MacDonald, William. *Believer's Bible Commentary.* Nashville: Thomas Nelson Publishers, 1995.

McGee, J. Vernon. *Revelation, Volume II.* Pasadena, California: Thru the Bible Books, 1979.

Moody Bible Commentary. Chicago: Moody Press, 2014.

NIV Archaeological Study Bible. Grand Rapids, Michigan: Zondervan Publishers, 2005.

Rogers, Adrian. *Unveiling the End Times in our Time.* Nashville: Broadman and Holman Publishers, 2004.

Ryrie, Charles Caldwell. *The Ryrie Study Bible.* Chicago: Moody Press, 2011.

Strauss, Lehman. *The Book of Revelation.* Neptune, New Jersey: Loizeaux Brothers, 1964.

Tenny, Merrill C., ed. *Pictorial Bible Dictionary.* Nashville: The Southwestern Company, 1975.

Tippit, Sammy. *Worthy of Worship.* Chicago: Moody Press, 1989.

The Baptist Hymnal. Nashville: Convention Press, 1991.

The United Methodist Hymnal. Nashville: The United Methodist Publishing House, 1989.

This Far by Faith. Minneapolis: Augsburg Fortress, 1999.

Vine, W. E. *An Expository Dictionary of New Testament Words.* Old Tappan, New Jersey: Fleming H. Revell Company, 1966.

Vines, Jerry. *I Shall Return*. Wheaton, Illinois: Victor Books, 1979.

Walvoord, John. *The Revelation of Jesus Christ.* Chicago: Moody Press, 1966

Wiersbe, Warren W. *Be Victorious*. Wheaton, Illinois: Victor Books, 1986.

Wiersbe, Warren W. *The Bible Exposition Commentary*. vol. 2. Wheaton, Illinois: Victor Books, 1989.

Wiersbe, Warren W. *With the Word*. Nashville: Thomas Nelson Publishers, 1991.

NOTES

NOTES